AS CLOSE AS THE TELEPHONE

AS CLOSE AS
THE TELEPHONE

The Dramatic Story of the Australian Life Line Movement

ALAN WALKER

ABINGDON PRESS
Nashville and New York

UNITY SCHOOL LIBRARY
Un
Lee's Summit, Missouri 64063

DISCARD

AS CLOSE AS THE TELEPHONE

Copyright © 1967 by Abingdon Press

All rights in this book are reserved.
No part of the book may be reproduced in any
manner whatsoever without written permission of
the publishers except brief quotations embodied in
critical articles or reviews. For information address
Abingdon Press, Nashville, Tennessee.

Library of Congress Catalog Card Number: 67-22168

Scripture quotations unless otherwise noted are from
the Revised Standard Version of the Bible, copyrighted
1946 and 1952 by the Division of Christian Education,
National Council of Churches, and are used by permission.

Scripture quotations noted Moffatt are from *The Bible:
A New Translation,* by James Moffatt; copyright 1935 by
Harper & Row.

SET UP, PRINTED, AND BOUND BY THE
PARTHENON PRESS, AT NASHVILLE,
TENNESSEE, UNITED STATES OF AMERICA

BV
656.4
W151a

CONTENTS

1

AN IDEA IS BORN

The Midnight Call

The clock had just struck midnight. It was Saturday night
and I was working late on the next day's preparation.
Suddenly the silence of our home was broken by the sharp
clang of a telephone ring.

"This is Roy speaking," said a quiet voice as I lifted the
receiver. "You don't know me, but can I speak to you for
a few moments? I apologize for so late a call.

"I have just written you a letter, which you will receive
on Monday morning. By that time I will be dead. I am
sorry to worry you, but there is no one who really cares

what happens to me and I would like to explain something to someone."

For over half an hour I pleaded with that would-be suicide, hoping some word would deflect him from his course of despair. I tried to get his name and address, but he would not go beyond his opening word—"Call me Roy." As he talked, some facts emerged. He was desperately lonely, he was in debt, he was in his own view a failure.

Failure! As the conversation came to a close I suggested that, before he took his life, he should come to the evening service in the Lyceum Theatre in Sydney. "It so happens I will be speaking on 'Life's Glorious Failures.' If you will come, God might speak to you through it all. Will you come?"

Suddenly the phone went silent; Roy was gone.

That Sunday night I stood up to preach with an added sense of drama and urgency. I looked over the sea of a thousand faces, wondering whether Roy was there. During the message I once referred to the possibility of his being present. "If you are here, Roy, please listen."

Back home that night the phone rang again. Sure enough, it was Roy, Roy Brown he now admitted. Yes, he had been in the audience that night. He had been helped in his thinking. He thought now he would be all right.

Still Roy refused to divulge his address. He accepted the suggestion of an appointment for 2:00 P.M. on Tuesday.

At 1:55 P.M. on Tuesday there was a call from the Darlinghurst police. The sergeant said, "We have found the body of a man named Roy Brown in a gas-filled room at King's Cross. On his chest was a letter addressed to you. Can you tell us anything about him?"

It was a pathetic letter. "I am afraid my faith has failed me. Please pray for me. I am terribly afraid. Suicide is not the easy way out, as many people believe. The pressure of the past few weeks has been too much for me. A job and £150 would have saved me, but I just don't believe I am worth it. I am a failure. I am leaving the world unwanted, unloved, and without hope."

Roy Brown, we discovered, was a thirty-eight-old Australian. An illegitimate child, reared by foster parents who later died, he had no one who seemingly cared whether he lived or died. For months he had been out of work. One by one he had pawned his possessions.

One remained. It was a stereophonic hi-fi. Neighbors said they used to hear him playing it for hours on end, especially one record he seemed to like: "Lonesome Road."

Now he had dropped behind on time payments for his stereo. A court case was threatened. It was the last straw. Roy Brown was not prepared to live without music.

So we buried him. There was no one who cared enough to come to his funeral. The Central Methodist Mission paid the undertaker. My wife and I were the only people present, and we had never even looked on his face. He died isolated and alone amid 100,000 at "The Cross," as alone as an early pioneer under a saltbush in the great Australian "never-never" country.

9

A Mantle of Safety

As alone as in an Australian desert! This very thought had its place in the evolving of an idea.

There was once a great Australian named John Flynn. "Flynn of the Inland," as he became affectionately known, went out in the early years of this century as a Presbyterian minister into Central Australia. There he discovered the intense isolation and loneliness of the pioneers, where in some cases a nearest neighbor would be five hundred miles away. He encountered the sorrows of loneliness among families far from medical assistance, among men and women who rarely saw another face.

Into the compassionate heart of John Flynn came the dream of casting a "mantle of safety" over the inland. With the coming of radio and the airplane, the mantle became a practical possibility. For long years Flynn labored until there stood in the scattered homes of the inland pedal wireless sets, and dotted at intervals across the land were the headquarters of the Flying Doctor Service.

Today a dream is a reality. Some of the terror of inland isolation is gone. Lonely homesteads are linked together for medical care, education, social intercourse, spiritual inspiration, by the miracle of radio. The bright shadow made by the wings of the protective planes of the Flying Doctors falls across the land. The "mantle of safety" is a fact.

Why not a "mantle of Christ" over Sydney? This was the idea that was born. Loneliness is not only of the stretching miles, it is also of the hurrying crowds. It not only belongs to distant places but belongs amid the impersonal people who inhabit the mass society of huddled cities.

A city is the loneliest place on earth. The larger the metropolis, the more people there are within its boundaries who are lost to their fellows, who live isolated, lonely lives, few caring whether they live or die. And Sydney is a big city, with the problems of a mass society deepening as it moves rapidly from its present population of two and a half to three million souls.

Many of us are fortunate; we live securely established within a family and kinship group. From our lives there run out into society lines which link us to others. In almost any need or problem we face, we know someone to whom we can turn who has the will and the skill to advise and help us. Never in our experience have we really faced a situation on the basis of our own isolated resources.

Many thousands of people around us share no such position of privilege. They may be living alone. They become caught up in a situation which they feel must be hidden from those nearest to them. They are poor, virtually without friends of influence who can guide and strengthen them. They belong to no supporting fellowship, such as the Christian church, in which a caring concern could express itself.

In society itself crucial changes have occurred. In smaller, rural communities there is a natural and inevitable knowledge of one another. Sometimes neighbors know too much! In a city physical closeness can go side by side with a canyon-like separation. Why, we scarcely know the names of our next-door-but-one neighbor, or the people

11

in the apartment above. Certainly we accept no responsibility for each other and rather cherish our independence.

The family physician once fulfilled an important role in the community. He became the confidant of many. In the privacy of his office or as he visited his patients, he dispensed much more than physical health. He was trusted with the inner secrets of many a life and home.

Now the family physician is becoming a person of the past. Panels of doctors service a community, and the personal relationship of the past becomes no longer possible. When one of our own children was sick recently, we had three different doctors who were in partnership come to our home in as many days. Under such circumstances a doctor becomes a doctor, no more.

In Sydney, half the population never goes to church. As a result, the Christian minister is no longer with half the people able to be a friend and pastor. People simply do not know where the minister lives, and would feel too embarrassed and awkward to go to his study or vestry even if they knew his address. Many people now would not want to be seen entering a church building or a minister's manse.

No one will ever be able to calculate the added suffering and misery in a community because people have lost touch with the Christian church. For nothing has developed to fill the vacuum that has emerged.

Where then do people turn in a crisis? The neighbor is a stranger, the doctor is but a name, the minister would not enter their calculations. So many a burden, which could be halved if shared, is carried alone. In a crisis, isolation can spell tragedy.

On December 23, 1964, the body of a woman, bearing the marks of malnutrition, was found in the room where she had lived alone. On a table next to her bedside was an open diary. On every page from January 1 of that year until the day she died were written the words: "No one came . . . no one came."

A mantle of safety over a city—how could it be achieved? In the Australian outback it was the radio and the airplane which bridged the physical separation. What could it be in a vast metropolis stretching from the Blue Mountains to the Pacific coastline, from Waterfall in the south to Palm Beach in the north? What would be within the reach of the rich and poor, of men and women, of young and old? How could a mantle of Christ be thrown over Sydney?

Help Is as Close as the Telephone

The telephone! It was the ringing of a telephone which supplied the key, and then all seemed plain.

Actually it was once again a call in the middle of the night which suggested the answer. One early morning at 2:00 A.M. the telephone rang. It was a woman, sobbing, on the other end of the line. It was in a way a simple problem she faced. Her husband was a commercial traveler. He was always absent in the country from Monday to Friday.

This particular week everything had gone wrong. One of the children became sick. The postman had brought a bundle of bills. "I cannot sleep," she said. "I've come to the end. I must speak to someone."

For half an hour she poured out her troubles to me, a

13

stranger. As emotion subsided I suggested she should go the next day to her neighborhood minister, whom she admitted she knew because he had performed her marriage ceremony years before. No, she refused to do this—"I would be too embarrassed to ask his help after all these years." Then, her friends might see her going to the rectory, and how could she be sure confidences would be kept?

"Why did you call me?" I asked. "I've seen you on television. And it is easy to talk on a phone—you can't see the tears trickling down my cheeks."

The advantages of the telephone were endless. The telephone was everywhere. Tens of thousands of homes across Sydney had a telephone. The red telephone box on the corner was within walking distance of most houses in the entire metropolis.

The telephone was impersonal yet intimate. People could remain anonymous if they wished. It was cheap—few could not afford a five-cent coin. It could provide a point of contact, and from a simple beginning endless follow-up could be attempted.

Suddenly the pattern became clear. There were running from telephones across Sydney hundreds of thousands of lines, and all could converge on one centre, one set of telephones where help could be offered. Along these thin lines could flow the joys and the sorrows, the spoken intimacies, the cries of despair of a million lives. The ubiquitous telephone became the instrument for the mantle of safety over Sydney.

What would happen if there were established a central

telephone reference centre? If a series of phones were staffed twenty-four hours a day, so that people would know they were always in reach of a friendly voice and a caring person, would they call? Would they trust a stranger if they knew that they could remain anonymous or that their confidence would be kept?

The answer seemed obvious and in the affirmative. Roy Brown called, didn't he? Then there was the woman pouring out her anxiety in the middle of the night. There were the countless other calls which came following radio talks and television appearances. Why should people not call?

Suddenly a vague idea became crystallized, localized. The Central Methodist Mission in Sydney owned a piece of land on the fringe of downtown Sydney. On it stood an old hall, one hundred years old. Dilapidated, derelict, it carried a plaque which read: "Wesleyan Day and Sabbath School, 1863." It stood on the main highway to Sydney's sports grounds; by it passed the buses to the airport. Scores of thousands of people would see it weekly.

There the telephone nerve centre could be built. There could be erected the counseling rooms for the cases requiring follow-through. There could be stored the resources to meet the inevitable calls which would come for physical relief. There could be established a great distributing centre for divine and human charity.

From such a centre there could indeed go forth the message to all Sydney, regardless of class or creed: "Help is as close as the telephone."

15

A Crucial Meeting

"Do you really think one church, however strong it may be, can take on its shoulders the burden of a city?" The speaker was one of the dedicated, wise members of the Executive Board of the Central Methodist Mission. The Board was debating whether it would make its next service project the setting up of a centre in Sydney which would say: "Help is as close as the telephone."

"The idea grips my imagination, but how could we do it? It would require a very large staff. The cost would be prohibitive. This is a project for the government, not for a single congregation of a church."

"You forget the untapped resources of Christian lay men and women," was the reply given. "I believe the telephones can be staffed by trained Christian volunteers who will eagerly grasp an exciting form of service to the people. From our own congregation and from other churches we will gain the people needed."

As with all dreams, there was needed the cold voice of realism which came that day. There could be no pulling back. Once the offer was made, we would be obliged to keep going. Five, ten, twenty years from now the telephones would still have to be staffed. Twenty-four hours a day, seven days a week, on workdays and holidays, someone must be at the phones.

Could we do it? Dare we attempt it? I asked for time. "Let the debate be adjourned. Let a handpicked group of people be called together. Let us gauge reactions. There is much being said and written about the laity of the church

16

becoming involved in the direct mission of Christ. But it remains a largely theoretical discussion. Most churches can supply few opportunities for service for their people. This will admittedly need scores, hundreds of people; but I believe they can be found."

Three weeks later, in our home at Roseville, the crucial meeting was held. Some thirty members of the Mission had been invited to discuss a new lay movement and commitment within the church.

I watched them as they arrived. They were the kind of cross section found in many churches. There were a bank officer and his wife, a nurse trainee, a school inspector, a personnel officer, a schoolteacher, a policeman, a carpenter, a laundryman and his wife, several business-men, a lawyer, several office girls, a public relations officer, a motor mechanic, and so on. In addition there were present the key staff members of the Mission.

As that crucial meeting proceeded, we all became con-scious of the leading of the Holy Spirit. One by one the obstacles were raised, and seemed to disappear. Gradually the group became fused into a unity. With a growing consensus came a quiet but sober enthusiasm. Not lightly did men and women commit themselves to a project which they sensed would demand long and wearing dedication. Yet all were gripped by the prospect of new opportunities for direct witness to the saving and caring power of Jesus Christ. Before the night was concluded, we knew we must go forward in faith.

From this initial and subsequent meetings emerged the main outlines of how the new telephone centre should be staffed, how assistance would be mobilized, and what training would be required.

First, a new precise lay movement should be established. Only people who became members of the movement would be permitted to serve. Demands would be definite and difficult rather than vague and easy. It would call for discipleship in depth from all who would seek to join.

Second, it would be a Christian movement. It would only accept people who confessed Jesus Christ as Savior and Lord. Members could come from any Christian denomination, but they must be Christian rather than merely humanitarian.

Third, training would be essential. Only people who had met training requirements could be accepted. After acceptance into the movement, refresher courses, attendance at periodic conferences and conventions would be an obligation.

Fourth, the movement would demand a disciplined membership. Applicants could not be accredited without interviews. All would be expected to accept tasks allotted. A periodic review of members would be undertaken, members being asked to remain active or resign.

It was also decided that training courses should commence at least nine months before the new Christian Service Centre opened. Only when there was prepared a voluntary team of at least one hundred people would we be ready for action.

Nothing proved more significant in the preparation of the mantle of Christ over Sydney than the decision to establish a new lay movement to staff the work. Without the existence of a trained, disciplined movement the Centre could not have carried the first thrust of responsibility, nor could the long, demanding haul of service over the months and years be endured.

We were surely led by the Holy Spirit when we planned the movement.

The Name: Life Line

Twelve months elapsed from the day the Central Methodist Mission Executive Board finally gave its approval to the opening of the telephone centre. It was a year of money raising and of training.

The Lord Mayor of Sydney at a meeting of professional and business men in the Sydney Town Hall launched a public appeal for $100,000, which was the sum required to erect the new Centre. For months the story was told in personal interviews soliciting donations, by mass media of radio, television, and the press. Slowly interest mounted and money flowed in. The government, the city council, several charitable foundations gave financial support. Gifts, large and small, were made. By opening date the appeal target was reached. Sydney had accepted a new idea.

It was in June, 1962, that the first training courses were held. Over 150 people enrolled at Sydney's College for Christians. There were three sessions held every Tuesday night:

6:30 to 7:15—Biblical lecture
7:15 to 8:00—Discussion groups
8:00 to 9:00—Course on counseling

Bible study passages were suggested. Book lists were provided for additional reading.

The major biblical lecture in the training course was entitled: "How Jesus Helped People." [1] Week by week the way Jesus faced human problems in his day was examined. Some of the titles were "Jesus and a Divorcée," "Jesus and a Suicide," "Jesus and a Prostitute," "Jesus and the Men Who Were Afraid," "Jesus and the Woman with an Incurable Disease," "Jesus and a Man with Spiritual Desires."

In the counseling course an attempt was made to equip telephone counselors with a rudimentary knowledge of some of the major human problems which they would face and basic principles of counseling. Telephone counselors were only contact people, but it was necessary for enough insight to be gained for an assessment of seriousness of need to be made. The breaking and broken home, the alcoholic, the compulsive gambler, the lonely, the depressive, the potential suicide, the man and woman in physical need would all be encountered. For these situations the training course was designed.

There came the day when the new project took a giant stride forward. The idea came that perhaps the new service could have its telephone number listed on the emergency page of the telephone directory with the fire brigade, ambulance, and other essential services. This, we realized, would lift the new Centre to a high level of

[1] Later published as *How Jesus Helped People* (Nashville: Abingdon Press, 1964).

public confidence. It also would mean that people could call from a public telephone without charge.

An approach to officials of the postmaster general's department brought firm refusals to the suggestion. There remained a further court of appeal. Perhaps the director general could be persuaded to grant the desired listing. A plane journey of five hundred miles to Melbourne seemed justified. When the director general learned that the telephones would be staffed twenty-four hours a day and during every day of the week he hesitated, saying, cautiously, it might be possible. Three days later the answer came: the new Centre would be listed as a personal emergency service in the next directory.

As opening day came near, there remained one serious unresolved issue: we could find no name that satisfied us. At first we had called it "Mantle of Christ." But in time we rejected this; it was too obviously religious and could frighten off some who would be most in need of assistance. "Christian Service Centre" was our next attempt. This was too tame, and besides a protest came from another organization which had already registered the name. This made it unusable.

It was a newspaperman who finally provided the name. One morning a newspaper report of a public meeting called to support the venture carried a heading: "Telephone Life Line." The moment of inspiration had come. It is to a sub-editor of the *Sydney Morning Herald* that Life Line owes its name.

So it was that all things were ready in March, 1963.

21

A new $100,000 building stood completed, a full-time staff of 10 people had been appointed, and 120 telephone counselors were trained and ready.

Life Line opened for business on Saturday, March 16, 1963.

2

LIFE LINE IN ACTION

The First Weekend

The Life Line telephones were opened at 5:00 P.M. on March 16, 1963. In the counseling rooms there was quiet tension. Would the people of Sydney accept our invitation? We had plunged $100,000 on an idea. Scores of people had prepared themselves for service. Four years of planning and praying and working lay behind Life Line. Would the telephones stand silent, unused?

The answer came at one minute past five o'clock. The phone in the central counseling room rang loudly. The counselor reached for the receiver: "This is the Life Line

Centre. Can I help you?" Life Line was in business.

So the telephones began to ring on that late Saturday afternoon in March. By midnight on the following day, 111 serious calls had been registered. With radio, television, and the Sunday press telling the story of the new round-the-clock service available to Sydney, the whole city seemed to sense something new had begun in its midst. Quite literally, the telephones began ringing on that opening day and they have not stopped since. Life Line has come to stay.

"In the last week I learned I have cancer, and have perhaps six months to live," said a quietly spoken voice of an early caller. "Can you say anything to help me?" The speaker was a young married man, thirty-five years of age, with two children.

"Every Monday morning," the sad voice continued, "I walk up the hill from my home to the school with the boys and leave them at the school. How can I go through with it on Monday? I know I will not be able to do it for much longer. Can you tell me anything of courage and faith? No one knows yet, not even my wife. I had to talk to someone."

It was a young counselor who took the call. Only recently had she come to know God as her Heavenly Father, Christ as her Savior. With simplicity, in hesitant, stumbling words she tried to explain the meaning of the love of God and the fact of eternal life.

It was a long conversation, the essence of it being faithfully recorded on the report forms of the Centre. Something must have happened in that conversation across

Sydney. The report ended with the word of gratitude spoken by the stricken man: "Thank you. I think I will now be able to walk up the hill on Monday with my boys tall and straight!"

In reporting this early incident from the files of Life Line let me say that all case material found in these pages is used with the permission of the persons involved or has been so disguised as to make sure that confidentiality so vital to a Life Line ministry is preserved.

Help is as close as the telephone. Life Line is planned to meet every form of human need. If within Life Line itself assistance cannot be given, then responsibility is taken to pass on the person to agencies where help can be found.

Little did we know how vast a sea of need lay beneath the affluent surface of Sydney. On this first weekend we realized we would be face to face with the whole gamut of human need. From plain loneliness to suicidal despair, from the tempted to the defeated, from the pathos of the unmarried mother-to-be to the breaking or broken home, from the abandoned child to the homeless man, from the doubting student to the faithless aged fearful of death the cry for help came.

It was before that first Saturday closed there came the first suicide call. It was from the manager of a city hotel. A boarder, drunk, had barricaded herself in her room saying she would, during the night, kill herself.

The manager was urged to try to persuade the woman to call Life Line on her room phone and speak to us. Within an hour the call came. She was the buyer in a fashion department in a large city store. Lonely, with no faith to live by, she could see no way out from her growing alcoholism but death.

A volunteer from Life Line spent the night with her, keeping final despair at bay. Psychiatric treatment followed over subsequent weeks. The day came when a confident, rehabilitated woman called at Life Line to express gratitude. "You did save my life," she said.

We made one serious miscalculation in planning. We hoped for unending telephone calls; we expected letters asking for aid. We did not anticipate the scores of people who came to the building seeking assistance. By car and taxi and in public transport they came, knocking on the door, seeking immediate assistance.

The climax came at midnight on the first Sunday. Two policemen were at the door. They had a man with five children, one a baby in arms, with them. Could Life Line provide food and accommodation?

The police had found the man wandering the streets. The night before, his wife had deserted him, leaving on the train for Sydney, three hundred miles from their country home. In panic he had bundled the children in the farm truck and had come to Sydney to find her. With little money and a crying baby of six months, what could he do?

In these early hours we were given a foretaste of what was to come. The city took us at our word. The people believed that help—any and every form of help—was as close as the telephone.

26

The Nerve Centre

The time is nine o'clock. It could be any morning of the week. Around a table a small committee is assembling for business. On the table are the reports on all who have called, visited, or written to the Centre in the previous twenty-four hours. The daily assignment committee settles down to work. It is the veritable nerve centre of Life Line.

Life Line has developed a simple but sufficient report system. As each telephone conversation continues, the counselor is taking notes. From this record the report form is completed. Behind the top portion of the report is a card which duplicates essential information later filed for quick reference.

All who come to the Centre are given a preliminary interview. The same report form is used, the information being gathered across a table rather than over a telephone. Letters are similarly summarized and transcribed to the report form.

Steadily the assignment committee works through the daily pile of reports. About 15 percent will be anonymous, so are simply filed—but filed carefully, for some valuable information could be there should that anonymous caller phone again, then giving a name.

Some of the reports need no further action. The telephone counselor has done all that was needed. Here, for example, is a story about a fourteen-year-old boy. He had rung at midnight the night before. His parents were out. He was alone. "I'm frightened," he said. "Can I talk to you for a few moments?"

27

Many call for follow-through. The committee discusses what should be done. Marriage guidance, financial advice, psychiatric help, employment, food or clothing assistance, help for an unmarried mother-to-be, spiritual counseling may be needed. Interviews are arranged with skilled and professional counselors and social workers.

At last the heavy task is done. The cards with the time allotted for interviews go to the central desk and switchboard. There they are filed in a huge rotary cabinet, readily available for reference when the repeat call comes. People whom the telephone counselor assesses require further assistance have been advised to call back after 11:30 A.M. on the day following their first call, by which time an appropriate appointment will be arranged.

Life Line has its own full-time staff of fourteen people. The director is an ordained Christian minister, skilled in pastoral counseling. A business manager handles the organization of the Centre. Social workers, receptionists, office secretaries, transport drivers, clothing supervisors handle the large business—of meeting the need of a city—which Life Line has become.

Some who could, and perhaps should, call for a counseling appointment fail to do so. Perhaps the telephone conversation has eased the tension. Perhaps circumstances change. Perhaps there is no desire to go beyond the somewhat impersonal, unrevealing telephone contact.

If, after some days, no follow-up call has come, a letter goes from the Director of Life Line offering assistance, inviting a further telephone call. Should nothing now happen, Life Line goes no further, except to file carefully the report form, knowing full well that some will be needed later when the pressure of necessity drives a puzzled or beaten person again to reach for the telephone. When that moment comes, be it day or night, the quiet voice of the counselor will say: "This is the Life Line Centre. Can I help you?"

"God never sleeps," says the Bible. Life Line gives to the city of Sydney the image of that kind of God, for it too, in his name, never sleeps.

The Telephone Counselor

The telephone counselors are the key to the success of Life Line. On the shoulders of the trained and dedicated volunteers who staff the phones falls the first thrust of the burdens of the city. Without them Life Line could not operate.

Telephone counselors are selected with great care. With some people who appear to be good prospective counselors, Life Line officers take the initiative and suggest attendance at lectures with a view that, if requirements are met, they will be accredited. With others who approach us, attendance at the next course of lectures is invited, it being emphasized that later interviews would determine whether they would be acceptable for nomination to the Life Line Movement and which form of service within the Movement would be offered.

The following steps must be followed by anyone who becomes accredited as a telephone counselor:

1. A full course of lectures must be attended: one on biblical and doctrinal subjects, one on counseling problems and Life Line procedures.
2. An interview or interviews with members of the Life Line Executive Board, where psychological and personality qualities are tested.
3. Where any doubt exists as to suitability, further interviews with professionally trained people.
4. Nomination to the Life Line Executive Board, where a majority vote for acceptance is necessary.
5. Sit-in sessions with experienced counselors at work on the telephone.
6. Where it is thought wise, an applicant is placed on a period of probation.
7. A service of dedication is held when the pledge of the Movement is publicly accepted and repeated.

Once accredited, the team is given careful oversight by the director. From the reports each counselor makes, an assessment of quality can be made. Often particular cases are discussed with the counselors to try to correct mistakes and improve efficiency. Through refresher courses, conventions, and periodic "live-in" conferences, attempts are made ever to lift standards.

Counselors come from a normal cross section of society. Businessmen, teachers, housewives, university lecturers, office secretaries, accountants, carpenters, nurses, lawyers, can be found among the counselors.

There are four counseling shifts daily. They run from 8:00 A.M. to 12:30 P.M.; 12:30 P.M. to 5:30 P.M.; 5:30 P.M. to 10:00 P.M.; 10:00 P.M. to 8:00 A.M. On the night session beds are available beside the phones for possible sleep between calls.

Every attempt is made to use counselors not more than twice a month. Life Line requires a long pull. We prefer counselors to retain enthusiasm. Overuse of any man or woman probably means a short rather than a long term of service.

Telephone counselors are required to work within a definite pattern of procedure. All must remain anonymous, for there would be endless danger in callers being able to contact counselors privately.

Beside the telephone which receives incoming calls in each counseling room is another, available always for the urgent outward call. It is necessary for the extensive referral system of the Centre. On call at all times is a designated senior staff member. Any serious problem which requires immediate action must be referred for decision. For example, no counselor is permitted to deal with a suicide situation without referral.

On the counselor's desk is a Life Line manual. In it are listed the directions under which all counselors operate. There are also listed some of the chief service agencies in the city to which, sometimes, reference is necessary. In readily available form are facts about Life Line which may be needed.

In the manual there are written the following "Twelve Rules of a Telephone Counselor":

1. The supreme purpose of the Life Line Centre is to lead men and women to Christ.

31

2. The weaving of people into therapy groups and into worship is part of the complete answer to much human need.

3. Treat every call as serious and genuine, yet be alert for the humbug and the hoaxer.

4. Record name and address of callers whenever possible.

5. Telephone counselors must at all times remain anonymous.

6. Careful and full written records are to be made from notes taken down during every telephone conversation.

7. Channel all action from calls as far as possible into the normal nine-to-five working day. Only in extreme emergencies envisage sending a "trouble team" during the night.

8. No action can be taken on the invitation of another person other than the one in need. It is almost impossible to aid someone who does not desire it.

9. Where possible, urge people to come to the Life Line Centre for interviews.

10. Counselors must not take action alone in answer to calls without consulting with Life Line staff members. Financial aid must not be given by counselors from their personal or Life Line resources. All assistance must be distributed through the Life Line organization.

11. A telephone counselor is a contact person; those in need must be referred to the appropriate division of Life Line.

12. Trust and expect the guidance of the Holy Spirit in every conversation and all counseling situations.

32

There are some who criticize the presence of nonprofessional telephone counselors in a counseling situation. It is a criticism without justification. Many people appear to be ready to discuss their problems with those who stand nearer to them in experience than with more highly trained professionals. Certainly many of the real, but simpler, human situations faced by Life Line would never reach the rooms of a professional counselor.

Always it must be remembered that telephone counselors, in a sense, are contact people. They are not without some training, and some have now built up valuable insights and skills after many months of service. But behind them is a referral system, and all cases requiring more than a telephone conversation are transferred to professional people capable of grappling with human need at a deeper level.

No one can question what the opportunity of telephone counseling has done in the lives of most who share in it. A new sense of purpose has been given to some. Others have come to grips with life in ways formerly unknown. Most have discovered through it a new meaning for Christian discipleship.

"I was overjoyed when notified that I had been chosen to be a telephone counselor," said one counselor after some months of service. "I know now that it was not until I had completed my first counseling call that I was really a committed Christian. The phone rang and I answered it for the first time, even then believing that I could help this man all on my own. I didn't get very far and after a few minutes he hung up.

"In a moment I knew where I had gone wrong. For the very first time in my life I faced God and pleaded with him to give me another chance. It was then that I gave my life to him and asked him to use it.

"I will never forget the experience I had during the next few minutes. The phone rang again and my prayer had been answered—this man had called again. We talked for a long time, and I found myself saying things that apparently he needed to hear, because finally he said that he thought he would be all right and hung up.

"Later that night, as I was about to leave for home, he called again and said: 'Don't worry about me—I'm all right now.' I knew then that I would be all right, too.

"The fact that God changes lives is very real to me," confessed the counselor, "because he certainly changed mine."

The Trouble Team

A trouble team is always on call at Life Line. Composed of two people, a man and a woman, it can rush into any situation demanding urgent action. Trouble teams can be credited with saving many lives.

Life Line is Sydney's suicide prevention centre. In common with the great cities of the world Sydney has a frighteningly high incidence of attempted and fatal suicides. Sometimes we think Roy Brown, with whose story we commenced, did not die in vain. His tragedy took its place in the planning and motive force which lies behind Life Line.

The Sydney Life Line Centre is equipped with three radio-controlled cars. From anywhere in Sydney, as they move on journeys of mercy, they are in direct contact with headquarters. In investigating suicide calls, radio has many times been crucial. It has made possible the quick summoning of ambulance or police, with the saving of life.

There was the case of the twenty-three-year-old man from Melbourne. Desperately lonely, just out of jail, with no money and no job, he called from a public phone. Disbelievingly, the counselor heard him say: "I thought I would be dead by now. Two hours ago I swallowed six razor blades. Perhaps I am not meant to die after all. Can you help me?"

A quick referral to the staff member on call brought authority to dispatch the trouble team. The button on the desk brought the devoted couple who live in the flat at Life Line headquarters into action. The radio car sped across the Harbour Bridge to Mosman. The casualty department of St. Vincent's Hospital was alerted to their coming. An X-ray proved the bizarre story to be true. Almost miraculously no serious damage was done. A week later the would-be suicide was discharged.

Trouble teams, like telephone counselors, are made up of volunteers who with Christian conviction and compassion contend for the lives and souls of the people. Several teams of two are composed of people who live at or near the Life Line Centre. Emergency reserve husband-wife teams are organized in various areas of the sprawling city. Sometimes because a call from a distant suburb has been answered by a nearby trouble team valuable time has been saved.

Principles for the operation of trouble teams have been built up from experience and are rigidly obeyed. It is perhaps the most risky service of all that Life Line attempts, and every effort is made to protect the two who, at any hour of day or night, might be called into action.

Life Line refuses to act on a "third party call." By this we mean that if a friend or neighbor or relative calls, asking for action, we do not respond unless the person directly concerned speaks to us. The reason for this requirement is obvious. We have no right to trespass, unasked, into another person's life or home. And anyway, no one can be really helped who does not ask for help.

There are, of course, exceptions. A boardinghouse proprietor called to say that one of his boarders had threatened to commit suicide; could Life Line send someone to help, quickly? Patiently the counselor explained that only if the boarder concerned called would a trouble team be dispatched.

"But he's already unconscious," shouted the distracted voice at the other end of the line.

Under no circumstances must a trouble team member go into a house alone. Two people, for protection's sake, must always operate together. A careful logbook is kept of times and destination and mileage of all trouble team journeys. Again, circumstances can arise where facts, verified facts, are vital.

Nothing is more dramatic in the Life Line story than its work in the area of suicide prevention. Always at the telephone is the consciousness that the next call could mean a matter of life and death. Always there is an overhanging atmosphere of urgency, for through Life Line lives can be saved—or lost.

A few miles from the heart of Sydney is Australia's most notorious scene for suicides. It is called "The Gap," and is a sheer drop of hundreds of feet to the wave-drenched rocks below. Rarely a week goes by without someone being dragged from the precipice edge. All too frequently there are those who crash to their deaths below.

There was one notable week when Life Line was used for the saving of three lives, one from The Gap. A woman, as she spoke of suicide, confessed, as her voice became thick and drowsy, that she had already taken a heavy overdose of tablets. Presently the phone became silent, and the counselor could hear what seemed to be the receiver knocking against the side of a table. The trouble team arrived just in time, testified the hospital to which the unconscious woman was rushed for remedial treatment.

A second witness to the power of the life wish which rises amid the death wish came from a young woman who called after she had sealed a room in her house and turned on all jets on the gas stove. Again, Life Line arrived just in time for a life to be saved.

The third incident involved The Gap. A distraught wife called to say her husband had left by car for The Gap, threatening to end his life. No such threat can be ignored. With The Gap, Life Line cooperates closely with the police. Owing to the possible need for people to be physically restrained, and the danger of a struggle developing on the cliff edge, Life Line always at once alerts the police. In this incident, Life Line and the police arrived together to find the man beyond the safety fence, seemingly preparing to jump to his death. Police restraint, Life Line friendship—and of course subsequent psychiatric treatment—restored a life and a home.

Drama is never far from the telephones at Life Line.

Life Line in Trouble

Life Line itself was in trouble, serious trouble. It happened early in its history. It could easily have destroyed public confidence.

The crisis burst with a telephone call from an officer in a government psychological clinic. "I have a serious charge to bring to your attention," he said. "I will be glad if you will make an investigation and let me know your conclusions before we go any further.

"I have a woman in my clinic who says she was raped last night by a Life Line officer who came to see her. She claims she called Life Line, after a quarrel with her husband, from a public phone. She spoke to a man who gave his name as ———.

"After an hour's conversation your counselor asked the woman to wait and he would come out to her and see what he could do. He arrived, picked her up, went to a lonely part of the road, and after further conversation, as dawn was breaking, attacked her."

Outrageous as the story sounded, there were some elements of it which suggested a knowledge of Life Line.

While realizing that the story was probably the fantasy of a disturbed woman, we initiated a searching inquiry.

Was there a report of any telephone call? Did the trouble team car show on its log any journey that night? Was a referral officer consulted over any case? What was the counselor's own story?

The night in question was one of the rare occasions when a counselor failed to arrive for the 10:00 P.M. to 8:00 A.M. all-night session. As was our custom, the phone was switched through to the Life Line flat where a couple on trouble team duty were spending the night.

Both husband and wife admitted that a call had come at the time claimed by the woman bringing the charge. A long conversation ensued, in the course of which the counselor admitted he had disclosed his name.

Had anyone driven out to Fairfield, the distant suburb where the woman lived? The answer was no.

Why was there no report form submitted? The counselor confessed that after the conversation he went to sleep, meaning to record the conversation next morning. When morning came, he had forgotten.

Could we prove no car had left the Centre? Fortunately we could. Car-log entries measured beside the speedometer showed no long journey could have been made. A careful check on the time factor verified that such a journey would have been impossible. Fortunately, under further questioning the woman's story collapsed. It was a case of projected sexual fantasy.

There are some who think procedures are applied too rigidly at Life Line. Incidents such as this show the need for care and protection. The counselor had broken two rules: he had failed to remain anonymous and he had not submitted a report of a telephone conversation. Both failures complicated inquiries and made the finding of an answer to a false charge more difficult.

Life Line, by its very nature, draws to itself some of the most disturbed and unbalanced people in the community. At any time false charges could break over its head. A full report system, the utter necessity of two people always moving together into situations, referral proceedings so that staff officers know what is happening are all essential.

Life Line, as it goes out to meet trouble, must protect itself and its staff from trouble.

Answers in Depth

Life Line supplies answers in depth to human problems. In the complexities of personal situations it is often necessary to move from level to level, and from one form of professional assistance to another. Life Line aims to follow through with people who turn to it for help.

The telephone counselor, as the contact person, supplies the first line of response to need. Many a conversation is sufficient in itself. As people unburden their minds and hearts, an easing of tension comes. As a discussion develops with a person objective to the situation, it frequently happens that people who call see some new angle to the problem they face. The dead-end street becomes a thoroughfare which in time leads beyond what looked like a complete impasse.

The Life Line counseling staff supplies the second answer in depth. Trained people in various fields, full-time and part-time, accept counseling appointments. Social workers, doctors, psychiatrists, marriage counselors, ministers work constantly at the Life Line Centre. Together they undertake scores, sometimes hundreds, of counseling interviews each month.

Behind Life Line are panels of professional helpers who in an honorary capacity are available to assist. Each man and woman on the particular panel undertakes to accept up to three cases at a time. There are five panels: doctors, psychiatrists, lawyers, youth advisors, business and financial advisors.

A third answer in depth lies in the referral agencies in Sydney. Life Line has no desire to duplicate what is being done adequately by others. Great use is, of course, made of government hospitals and psychiatric services. The closest cooperation between Life Line and the several admission centres for the mentally and emotionally disturbed has been established.

No attempt, for example, has been made to establish a clinic or centre for alcoholics. Alcoholics Anonymous, the Salvation Army, the Sydney City Mission, and the Langton Clinic all are at work in this field. Life Line refers to one or other of these centres the alcoholics who come for assistance.

A fourth level of response is given through the various residential institutions operated by the churches and the state in Sydney. Hospitals, children's homes, homes for the aged, hostels for students, night refuges for the homeless, are all listed at Life Line. To them are channeled those who need to be lifted from their environment into some form of custodial care.

With many a case, cross-reference of persons is necessary. More than one specialist is needed to grapple with the complicated situation which has developed.

A compulsive gambler rang Life Line. Over a period of three years he had squandered $6,000 on the slot machines. Now a climax of crisis had been reached. Friends who had loaned him money were threatening legal action. His wife had discovered the loss of their savings. As a consequence, she had declared their marriage was at an end. He used the word "suicide," for he could see no other way out of the disaster which had overtaken him.

What could he do? A financial advisor showed how he could combine all his debts, take a second mortgage on his house, and pay them off. The mortgage could be discharged, in the light of his income, in three years of hard saving.

A marriage counselor grappled with the home that was in jeopardy. Seeing a new concern in the husband, the man's wife showed the grace of forgiveness. She offered to seek part-time employment so they could grapple with debt together.

A psychiatrist had first come to grips with the deep depression which had settled over the man's mind. Gradually the threat of suicide receded as a way forward emerged.

Spiritual counsel resulted in a new understanding of the love and patience of God. An alternative to the time spent in the slot machine club had to be supplied. It was found in a neighborhood church where the whole family became linked in fellowship and in worship.

Here was seen in action the depth response of Life Line. All this was necessary for one man, one home. To see a life rehabilitated and a home restored justified it all. Life Line does supply answers in depth to human need.

The Central Methodist Mission

Life Line is an agency of the Sydney Central Methodist Mission. As a result, there stands behind it the strength of what can be justly called one of the strongest evangelistic and service centres in all the world.

The Central Methodist Mission is Australia's oldest and largest Methodist church. It is the central city church of Methodism in Sydney. In addition to its widespread evangelistic ministry, the Mission is notable for two features in its policy. It undergirds the preaching of the Christian gospel by extensive fellowship and group activities and by a series of fourteen social service agencies and institutions.

There are, under the roofs of the homes, hospitals, and hostels of the Mission, 730 people each night of the year. There is a full-time staff of 260 under the direction of the Mission. The annual budget of the Mission exceeds one million dollars.

Life Line is greatly strengthened by being part of so large a church organized to meet human need. Doors can be opened quickly within the one organization which would take much longer if other agencies, with their rightful priorities, had to be approached.

The Central Methodist Mission directs three children's homes, giving custodial care to 140 children. The Sydney Night Refuge and Men's Hostel is an agency of the Mission. Here homeless men can find a refuge. Six cubicles are kept in reserve for Life Line. A call to the manager up until 10:30 P.M. opens the door for a man in urgent need of accommodation.

Waddell House is Australia's first Christian psychiatric hospital. It is a 42-bed hospital directed by the Mission. The psychiatrists of Waddell House fulfill a vital role in Life Line. One psychiatrist is always on roster to take an urgent case. Waddell House, in some senses, fulfills the purpose of a psychiatric clinic for Life Line.

The five homes for the aged operated by the Mission are graded to meet the needs of senior people at the various stages of their need. Frank Vickery Village is composed of cottages for couples and single units in which people care for themselves. Hoban House and the W. G. Taylor Home provide full accommodation and board for men and women, with nurses on the staff. Sunset Lodge is available virtually as a convalescent home, where residents of the other homes may be transferred when bed-ridden with some temporary illness which demands full nursing care.

Lottie Stewart Hospital is a long-term hospital of 114 beds. All who enter its doors are confined to their beds. For most it is a terminal hospital, where compassionate care is offered until the end.

At the heart of the Central Methodist Mission stands Wesley Centre, from which the Mission is administered and in which the group dynamic policy of the Mission is expressed. Opened in 1966 at a cost of two million dollars, it stands in the heart of downtown Sydney.

Many groups operate within Wesley Centre. There are extensive youth activities. There meet within the Centre a whole series of special interest or age groups: the Business Women's Group, Crossways Club for men, International Club, Young Adults Group, Young-Marrieds Group, Couples Club, and Senior Citizens Fellowship.

To these various groups people who turn to Life Line in loneliness and isolation are directed. Fellowship is one of the deep needs of a mass society. By care in introduction and integration many a lonely person, lost in the heartless city, has found new friends and learned to say the necessary phrase "I belong" in the group activities of Wesley Centre.

As part of the Wesley Centre there has been established the Wesley Club. It is virtually a Christian club in which over two thousand people find a centre for meeting and activities of interest. The club offers many facilities to its members: lounges and foyers, library and reading rooms, conference and activity rooms, games and billiards section, shower and change rooms, eating and dining facilities.

Life Line is immeasurably enriched because it is part of the Central Methodist Mission. From the Mission and its various centres comes much of the ability of Life Line to offer answers in depth.

The Art of Caring

The Good Samaritan, in the famous parable Jesus told, cared for a man stricken on the Jericho road until he was well. He began with first aid by the roadside. He then placed him on his own donkey and walked beside him to the nearest inn. He paid for his care; then, on leaving, gave money to the innkeeper and said: "Take care of him; and whatever more you spend, I will repay you, when I come back" (Luke 10:35).

Life Line seeks to express the art of caring. It offers first aid, but it recognizes that many people need friendship and help long after an immediate crisis situation has passed, beyond the aid that can be given in face-to-face counseling situations. Therefore it has mobilized and trained a group of volunteer lay men and women who promise to assist through the expression of concern and friendship in the rehabilitation of those needing it.

There are many who need follow-through assistance. There are the alcoholics and the compulsive gamblers who face a long struggle, with the frequent temptation to lapse, if inner freedom is to be found. There are those who, in the depth of depression and despair, have attempted to commit suicide. The mists of depression are almost certain to fall again, even if not as black and impenetrable as in the moment when death seemed the only way. There are the lonely whose loneliness turns them in upon themselves, perpetuating and deepening the isolation and the suffering. There is the unmarried mother who after the birth and adoption of her child requires

46

understanding and friendship. There is the person with spiritual desires who finds it hard to enter, perhaps for the first time, the fellowship of the church and to walk the way of life of a Christian.

"Carers" fill a very vital role in the work of Life Line. As with telephone counselors they are obliged to attend lectures, to be interviewed, and are accredited for the task. It is their privilege to keep in touch with someone allocated to them for approximately three months. By telephone conversations, letters, meetings, proof is given that somebody cares.

The "Caring Division" has its own secretary, to whom names go from the Life Line Director. Every attempt is made to link together people with some compatibility. Young people care for young people, notice is taken of educational and cultural standards, and employment interests are taken into account.

As Christmas came near in 1965, an old man of seventy called Life Line. Living alone, frail, he faced the future with fear. As a young man he had broken from his family and had seen nothing of his three brothers and a sister since. Could Life Line do anything to help him?

A member of the Caring Division went out to see him. She found him sitting on the veranda in his little home. Sensing how deep was his desire to be linked again with his family, she set out, unknown to the old man, to try to discover whether the brothers and sister were still living. The electoral roll and the telephone directory were her starting points. Steadily she began calling every person with the same surname in the directory. At last a man admitted he had heard his father speak of a lost brother. He was a nephew. With a firm clue the rest of the search became easy. A letter to Brisbane and a visit to an address in Sydney established contact with the brother and sister who still lived.

At last, armed with her facts, a delighted "carer" broke the news that a family had been found. Before Christmas there took place a unique family reunion in that little home in Sydney, and the friend from Life Line who had made it all possible was present.

"Caring is the thing," once wrote G. K. Chesterton. "Caring matters most."

Group Therapy

Life Line has made a start, but only a start, in the area of group therapy. Obviously the opportunities and the need to supply supportive assistance through group participation are almost endless.

There is really not much difference between people. We are all born with the same basic drives and desires; we all face the same kind of temptations and experiences. Yet so often we imagine the situation with which we must grapple is unique, peculiar. We fail to realize that others around us struggle as we do, knowing the same defeats and victories, the same joys and sorrows, which we know.

All this is especially true amid the inner failures of human personality. The shame and despair of the alcoholic are common to alcoholics. The thoughts and actions of compulsive gamblers are largely alike among all who have lost the freedom not to gamble. The feeling of helplessness and contrition which overwhelms the homosexual or even the person grappling with problems of masturbation or any form of abnormal sexuality are common to all in whose lives sensuality becomes a tyranny.

Somehow, however, this fact escapes us. We think, especially with secret thoughts and habits, that no one else is like us. We suffer, often in silence and in self-condemnation, imagining that no one faces what we face.

Group therapy supplies the answer. Alcoholics Anonymous is successful precisely because people facing similar inner struggles for deliverance find they fight not alone. The sharing of aspirations and problems, the recounting to each other of stories of defeat and victory, is itself a therapy. To be part of an accepting fellowship, where all fears of judgmental attitudes are dissolved, is itself a liberating experience.

A "New Life Group" operated as a part of Life Line for a period. Into the group were introduced people with varying personal problems, such as alcoholism and chronic depression. We believed there might be value in establishing such groups, rather than gathering together people all facing the same inner conflicts and defeats.

Today, policy has changed. Specialist groups are operating. A regular meeting of unmarried mothers is held where, before and after the birth of the child, the coming to grips with the thoughts and emotions of those involved is attempted. Doctors, social workers, a psychologist, a minister, share in the leadership as one by one the physical,

49

psychological, and spiritual needs of the unmarried are faced.

Two Gamblers' Liberty Groups meet weekly for compulsive gamblers. Again with three or four leaders, gamblers, together with wives or husbands of those grappling with this form of inner bondage, share their experiences and struggles. Between meetings members know how to contact one another, and twenty-four hours a day they know they can talk with the Life Line counselors.

Group therapy is offered to lonely, anxious, and fearful people through the various groups at Wesley Centre. Here every attempt is made to assimilate a new member, without every member of the group knowing that the new member has come through Life Line. There is need for normal, healthy relationships in many cases, and interest and activity within a group small enough for members to have a sense of belonging is what is required.

The Therapy of Worship

If you were to walk into the foyer of the Lyceum Theatre on a Sunday night in Sydney, you would see two people wearing a few inches of red ribbon on their lapel or dress. They would be representatives of Life Line, waiting for people who are coming to worship perhaps for the first time, because of an invitation from Life Line.

Life Line is unashamedly Christian and church related. Only people who accept Christian commitment and allegiance may become accredited in telephone counsel service and in the Caring Division. While religion is not forced on anyone, counselors are encouraged to seek the moment when the name of God is mentioned. If at the end of a conversation on the telephone it becomes natural to suggest a prayer, then to pray with a caller can set a personal problem in a new context.

There is none of the timidity which is found in some Christian undertakings, as though it is permissible to talk about anything save that which matters most, the love and power of God. So many problems, on whatever level they begin, should end in the presence of God. For only in the context of a religious interpretation of life can lasting answers be found.

Worship is the best therapy of all. A group of American hospital chaplains, as quoted by Dr. Howard Clinebell in *Mental Health Through Christian Community,* say: "Twenty centuries witness to the effectiveness of . . . worship in changing men's lives for the better, in bringing release from guilt and freedom from fear, in giving direction and purpose to their striving, and in lifting them out of neurotic self-concern into healthful and creative relationships to their fellows." [1]

Hence attempts are made to lead men and women into the experience of worship. Where links are already established, encouragement is of course given to maintain and strengthen them.

Many of the people who turn to Life Line out of an

[1] "American Protestantism and Mental Health," *Journal of Clinical Pastoral Work,* I (1948), 1; quoted in Clinebell, *Mental Health Through Christian Community* (Nashville: Abingdon Press, 1965), pp. 56-57.

experience of need have lost all relationships with the Christian church. Some may be separated by two or three generations from any Christian knowledge or practice. For these, to attend an act of public worship represents a bold and difficult step. For these, worship in a theater, as is offered week by week in the Sydney Central Methodist Mission, can be an easier starting point. With lay men and women organized to greet newcomers, to sit with them, to assist in assimilation, it is to worship in the Lyceum Theatre that people are invited.

Sunday after Sunday, people come to worship from Life Line. Telephone counselors, personal counseling, and therapy groups have been instrumental in introducing them to the experience of worship. And often, when the climax of worship on a Sunday night is reached and opportunity is given for an open commitment to Christ to be made, someone from Life Line comes forward. Then can come the end of that estrangement from God from which so much of the disharmony of life arises. Peace is made with God.

Recently I was on a lecturing tour in a northern New South Wales town. As I left the local radio station after making a broadcast, the radio announcer, who had introduced me, slipped a generous donation into my hand: "It's for Life Line," he said.

"At the end of my tether, I was forced a year ago to take an extended holiday. But it was more than a holiday I needed. After several weeks in Sydney I found I had merely carried my problems with me. Desperate, I rang Life Line.

52

"During the next week I was given an appointment with a Christian psychiatrist, one on the Life Line panel. Several sessions followed, and gradually I began to find wholeness and sanity again.

"I began on a Sunday night to attend worship at the Lyceum Theatre. At last I was ready to respond to the call of God which I had begun to hear. I made a full commitment to Christ. That night my life was changed. I found a peace which for years had been unknown. I believed Life Line led me to God. I would do anything in my power to extend the work and influence of Life Line."

With all too few people is the climax of God-discovery reached. When it happens, there is more than joy "in the presence of the angels of God"; there is a deep satisfaction in all who work and pray for Life Line—for its ultimate purpose has been achieved.

3

THE LIFE LINE MOVEMENT

The Sleeping Giant of the Church

If you were to ask me what is the most startling discovery which has come with Life Line, I would not begin speaking of the volume of need uncovered in a city. I would not name one or another human problem. Rather, I would tell of the amazing enthusiasm, dedication, renewal which have been seen in the lay men and women who voluntarily serve Life Line. The most important development which has occurred among us is the founding and the growth of the Life Line Movement.

There is a great awakening taking place in the Christian church around the world. It is the awakening of the laity. We are seeing now the abysmal wrongness of what Emil Brunner has called "the minister church." Because the proclamation of the gospel has been left largely to the ordained priest and minister, because the laity has seen itself largely in a passive role in the life of the church, the world mission of Jesus has faltered.

The concept of the total ministry of Christ we must now grasp. Ministers and lay men and women have their own tasks to fulfill, but it is one task and one ministry. It is convenient to Christ in his church to have ministers who by their training and their full-time availability can carry out specific duties within the life of the church. But there is no difference in kind between the ministry of the ordained clergy and the laity. All are one in Christ; all make up the total ministry of Christ in the world.

The desire of countless lay Christians is to share directly in evangelism and service. The regular worship of God, the maintenance of the organization of the church, the raising and giving of money have been carried on faithfully by millions of devoted Christians. Yet in an inarticulate way there has been the sense of something missing. That something has been direct, personal involvement in witness and in service for Christ in the world.

There is a grievous weakness in much that is being written about the role of the laity. It is all so theoretical. The blunt fact is that in the present structure of local churches there is not enough for the laity to do in direct evangelism and service. There are the usual tasks which must be undertaken in Sunday schools, in the running of worship, in committees, in house-visitation evangelism. In some churches, such as the Methodist, there are opportunities for lay preaching.

When these tasks have been listed, what then? There remain hosts of people whose enthusiasm has not been kindled, whose personal dedication has not been won.

The Christian education programs of the churches often languish and training programs win few enrollments. Why? Because it is Christian education and training with no immediate object in view. It is almost training for training's sake, and this wins but a limited allegiance.

I wonder how many applicants a business house would get if it advertised in general for people to apply for employment? It is precisely because an advertisement lists openings for a manager, an accountant, a sales representative, a stenographer, that the response comes. It is because a commercial enterprise does not try to find jobs for people, but people for jobs, that staff requirements are met.

The "sleeping giant of the church" will awaken when the role of the laity is more specifically defined. It will come when the structure of the church is modified so as to use the followers of Christ in direct witness and service in the church and in the world.

Nine months before the opening of the Life Line Centre the Life Line Movement was established. Undoubtedly, apart from the initial concept of Life Line itself, it is the most important thing which has happened to us.

The Life Line Movement shows what happens when the laity of a church comes alive.

The Pattern of a Movement

At the heart of the Central Methodist Mission in Sydney is the Life Line Movement. It was established in June, 1962, as an all-embracing challenge to "discipleship in depth" in the cause of Christ. The purpose of the Movement is fourfold: to call to personal holiness of life, growth in Christian knowledge, dedication to service, and witness in society.

Membership in the Movement is open to all who are members of any of the branches of the Christian church and who are ready to accept the pledge and discipline.

The pledge of the Life Line Movement represents a fivefold spiritual commitment. It is:

1. I accept Jesus Christ as my Savior and Lord.

2. I seek, by personal piety and corporate prayer, to grow in holiness and to be a channel of God's grace.

3. I seek to grow in Christian knowledge through Bible study, weekly attendance at Sunday worship and such training courses as may be available from time to time.

4. After consultation, I accept the place and service to which I may be appointed in the Life Line Movement.

5. I agree to abide by the rules of the Life Line Movement.

No one can become a member of the Movement who does not fulfill its basic requirements. First, an application must be made and registration be completed for a course of training lectures. Second, a personal interview is necessary with members of the Executive Board of the Movement so that an assessment of personal qualities can be undertaken. Third, there is nomination and acceptance at a general meeting of the Movement. Fourth, a service of dedication is held when a public declaration of the pledge is made before the members of the Movement.

The Life Line Movement accepts within its membership people from all the major Christian churches. At first it was composed predominantly of people who were worshiping members of the Central Methodist Mission. As news of the Movement spread, so did the range of applications for membership.

"I am the secretary of a Roman Catholic organization in Sydney," said an attractive young mother who one day came to the Life Line Centre. "We feel we are not doing enough in Christian service and have looked for somewhere to offer assistance. Our members are more excited by Life Line than anything else we have found. Would you allow a group of Roman Catholics to join the Movement?"

Would we? It was a new departure, but there was no hesitation in our response. The new spirit focused and released by Pope John and the Ecumenical Vatican Council was working miracles in church relationships in Sydney. Here was the evidence of it, and we rejoiced.

The day came when, after attendance at lectures in Wesley Chapel, after repeating the pledge, the first Roman Catholic group of people was accepted for telephone

58

counseling service at Life Line. The Movement was certainly going places!

The Life Line Movement is bigger than the Life Line Centre. Since the Movement is a company of people committed to "discipleship in depth," its members find many tasks in a church like the Central Methodist Mission. The goal is to enroll in the Movement all who serve the Mission and its various agencies and activities.

There are four main divisions in the Life Line Movement. There are the Telephone Counseling Division, Caring Division, General Service Division, and the Wesley Centre Division. Each division has its own tasks, which in turn determine the nature of training courses.

Someday the sleeping giant of the church, the laity, will awaken. Then the world will indeed witness another great era of Christian renewal. How do we know? In one small area of the church's life we have seen it happen.

Nothing more important over these years has happened to us than the emergence of the Life Line Movement.

A Training Program

There is movement, interest, almost excitement, around the entrance to the Wesley Centre auditorium. It is Tuesday night, an opening night for a new series of training lectures for the Life Line Movement at Sydney's College for Christians. Around the tables are scores of people registering for the series. Names, addresses, church affiliations are being recorded, together with the courses elected for study.

The College for Christians is the adult Christian education program of the Central Methodist Mission. Planned to meet the needs of a downtown city church, lectures begin early at 6:30 P.M., so that people wishing to attend after the day's work in the city may do so without undue delay.

A twenty-minute devotional opening begins the evening sessions. Hymns, a period of intercession when people present may voice their prayers, an emphasis on sharing and fellowship supply midweek spiritual nourishment.

For effective Christian service, training must be received in two major areas of knowledge. First, there must be a growing understanding of the Christian faith, of doctrine, of the Bible. How can there be an expression of Christ if we do not come increasingly to know the mind of Christ?

Second, there is need for training in the particular subjects and disciplines where the service is to be rendered. In human relationships and problems it is an awareness of the mental and emotional processes of people which is needed. There must also be training in the principles which govern the form of service to be rendered.

The Life Line training program has always a series of lectures which are based on the Bible. The two courses which have been most successful are entitled: "How Jesus Helped People" and "How Jesus Cares." The former series has been published in England and America, and the book is used as a textbook for Life Line applicants.

Over the months titles of other series have included: "Christian Mission in a Mass Society," "How to Be a

Christian," "Understanding the Lord's Prayer," "Caring Through the Bible," "Christ, a Man of the World," "How to Believe," and "The Many-Sided Cross of Jesus."

Following the first lecture the college breaks up into ten discussion groups. The lecturer, in addition to issuing a précis of the lecture given, prepares five questions for group discussion. Under skilled leaders the opportunity is given for all to express themselves on the theme of the lecture they have just heard.

Each group is invited to record its answer in one sentence to one of the questions. At the end of the discussion period all reassemble, and from the groups the recorded answer is given.

At 8:00 P.M. each Tuesday at least two lectures are offered. One is an initial course for new people seeking to join the Movement. The other is a refresher or more advanced series of lectures for members of the Movement.

The subject material covered in the initial course is indicated in the following lecture titles:

"Life Line—Its Nature and Purpose"
"The Art of Caring"
"Marital Disharmony"
"The Problems of Youth"
"The Psychologically Disturbed"
"The Physiological Aspects of Alcoholism"
"Handling Social Distress"
"Pitfalls and Triumphs"
"Practical Do's and Don't's"
"Counseling to Spiritual Need"
"The Centrality of Conversion"

In the more advanced courses a whole series is devoted to one of the human problems which most frequently come to Life Line. Lecture series are given on alcoholism, compulsive gambling, marriage counseling, the emotionally disturbed, suicide, social case work, and problems of the teen-ager.

The Life Line Movement expects to see growth in the life of its members. It is not a case of once a Life Line member, always a member.

At the assignment committee meeting members are alert for weaknesses or revealing mistakes in the reports submitted by counselors. The director keeps in close touch with counselors, speaking as much as possible with each one while on duty. Where it is considered necessary, counselors are invited to come to the Centre for an interview with the director who carefully but firmly discusses weaknesses in counseling which he or the staff have discovered.

A newer development is based on the team concept. Counselors are grouped under a strong leader who keeps in touch with each member of his group. It is his task to detect emotional difficulties in the lives of counselors and to watch for any departure from the standards and procedures of counseling.

In-service training is a feature of the ongoing planning of the Life Line Movement. All-day conferences and weekend "live-in" conventions are held at intervals. Book lists are circulated to stimulate reading. In other words, every effort is made to encourage members to go on growing in knowledge and efficiency in service.

A yearly family camp in a conference centre near Sydney has become a feature of the Movement. In a weekend of living together, with children cared for during lecture and sharing sessions, links are forged, confidence is strengthened, spiritual dedication is deepened. Life Line through such experiences is becoming a serving fellowship of richness and joy.

A Crisis in Discipline

"I am writing to resign from the Life Line Movement," were the opening words of an angry letter which one day came to the office. "I resent the kind of letter received this week and want nothing more to do with you or the Movement."

The letter was the first of several letters and telephone calls which revealed that something of a crisis had come. The cause was a communication sent to all members some months after the opening of the Centre. It was an early attempt to express a note of discipline in the affairs of the Life Line Movement.

Life Line, as with all new ideas and movements, brought its flood of enthusiasm. As the first adventure and excitement of service subsided, a slackness crept into counseling procedures. Several mistakes were made because telephone counselors were either ignorant of the methods of the Centre or deliberately took their own course of action.

To counter the weakness which had appeared, all members were urged to attend a refresher course. A little later an all-day convention was held. As so often happens, the ones most in need of inspiration and guidance were absent.

The letter which caused offense followed. Bluntly we stated that if telephone counselors were not prepared to grow in knowledge and efficiency, if they were not ready to attend follow-up lectures from time to time, resignations would be welcomed.

Well, we got our resignations. Christians had not been used to this kind of discipline. As often happens in churches, anything goes. The church is expected to be grateful for any service that is offered and given, and always, as it is unpaid service, gratitude is the only response that is expected.

But why? Why should not the service offered to Christ be more demanding than work that is done primarily for money? There is a revealing comment in the Moffatt New Testament Commentary on the first chapter of Galatians. Dr. George S. Duncan says: " 'Servant' is an inadequate translation. . . . The 'bond-servant of Christ' is not free to offer or withold his 'service'; his life is not his own, but belongs entirely to his Lord." [1]

A careful roll is kept of attendance at all lectures and conferences. If, over a period of time, members of the Movement do not share in ongoing development, an approach is made to the laggard member.

The discovery we have made is that people are ready, apart from the few exceptions, to accept the demands of a disciplined movement. In the service of Christ I am

[1] George S. Duncan, *The Epistle of Paul to the Galatians*, "The Moffatt New Testament Commentary" (New York: Harper & Row, 1934), pp. 21-22.

sure we ask not too much but too little of people. It is not easy to be accredited into the Movement, so it is a valued privilege. It demands consistency in devotion and continual growth to stay in the Movement, and most people are glad to accept its standards.

There is after all a great gladness in being a "bond-servant" of Jesus Christ and meeting God in your neighbor.

Telephone Counselors

Telephone counselors have to be ready for anything. When the phone rings, it could be a simple case of loneliness; it could be the occasional hoaxer; it could be a matter of life and death.

"I am in great trouble; can you help me?" There was urgency, agitation in the voice of the caller. Who was he? What was his story? There had been a tragic double murder; two bodies were found on the banks of the Hawkesbury River. A suspect was cornered in a house on the outskirts of Sydney. The police moved in for the arrest. As, with guns drawn, they approached the house, the inmate called Life Line: "Can you please help me?"

Another day a friend of a man serving a term in prison called, requesting unusual assistance. The prisoner had one possession he cherished above everything else: his dog. News had come to him that the dog, being cared for at a country town named Wagga Wagga, had disappeared. Could we do anything to find it? The telephone counselor, himself a policeman it so happened, had a friend at Wagga Wagga. An approach to him began a search for the dog.

The day came when Life Line was able to write to a man in prison, telling him his dog had been found and was being looked after till his discharge.

Simple, dramatic human stories such as these pass through Life Line week by week. Behind them are people, just people, who need a friend, who, knowing not where to turn, turn to Life Line. In the often unnamed name of Christ, need is met.

Telephone counselors are obliged to follow the instruction manual issued to them. Specific guidance is as follows:

OPENING SENTENCE

"This is the Life Line Centre. Can I help you?"

VOICE

Speak strongly so people can hear, yet with friendship and understanding.

LISTEN

Be a good listener.

Make comments to keep conversation going and open up the problem.

Remember: just to allow people to talk will often mean great help is given.

RECORD CONVERSATION

Begin writing notes at once, on scribbling pad, giving no indication you are doing so.

Record all information possible.

REPORT FORM

After each conversation fill in report sheet from notes and memory.

Write legibly and fully.

Indicate if you think the case gives the opportunity of follow-up by the staff.

GETTING OF NAME

Attempt during conversation to get name, address, phone number of caller. Do not be discouraged if some desire to remain anonymous.

Still make full report.

FOLLOW-UP

Where follow-up is necessary do *not* arrange for an interview.

Ask the caller to call back next day.

Indicate what you have done on the report sheet.

EMERGENCY VISITS

No promise for an immediate trouble team visit is to be made without reference to senior staff member. If serious emergency, call (at any hour) the staff member "on call" for that day or night.

THIRD PARTY CALL

Make no promise to call or approach another person on the request of a caller. For example, for Life Line personnel to call a husband because a wife requests it only causes resentment.

UNSHOCKABLE

Be unshockable over what you hear.

Do not sit in moral judgment on anyone.

MEDICAL OR PSYCHIATRIC HELP

Where there is evidence of a condition requiring medical or psychiatric treatment, find out whether the caller is under treatment from any other doctor, psychiatrist, or hospital and record the name of the doctor and hospital.

SPIRITUAL COUNSEL

Be eager to introduce God and Christian truth into telephone conversations, yet do not force religious faith upon people. Remember: without God there is nothing to say in many human situations.

The director of Life Line is the pastor of the counselors. During each shift throughout the day the director makes it his business to visit the counseling room. Staff members often, out of office hours, call the counselor on duty so there is no sense of being alone. Where there is anxiety over the adequacy of response to need, encouragement is given to share concern rather than carry it. There is a price to be paid for accepting something of the sin and sorrow of a city.

The Caring Division

The central purpose of the Life Line Caring Division is to offer friendship. Through wise, strong, continuing understanding, doorways to a new life can be opened.

There is also need for acceptance. No mental or emotional suffering is more acute than that caused by feelings of rejection. To sense the moral condemnation of others, to be exiled from personal, family, or group relationships, is to be often plunged into despair.

There is need for stability. Many people have built up inner conflicts and outer confusions over the years which cannot be resolved overnight. They require time, patience, love, if recovery is to be complete.

The Caring Division has become second in importance only to the telephone counselor as a feature of Life Line. With its own course of lectures, its full-time secretary, its executive meetings where "carers" are matched with people needing rehabilitation, it fulfills a far-reaching ministry.

There is many a pitfall in the business of caring. No one dealing with people, especially people in distress, can escape the risks which go with establishing human relationships.

From our past experience in the art of caring, members are issued the following advice:

Be skeptical. Probe into the stories given you. Look for possible contradictions and discrepancies. You will not help a person if you are gullible and foolishly sentimental.

All gifts of money or clothing should be distributed through Life Line. If people need physical or financial help, let Life Line staff members deal with it.

Be on guard against the compromising situation. Do not spend time alone in the room of a member of the opposite sex. Remember the peril which can arise from false charges and fantasy.

Do not allow people to become too attached to you as a person or too dependent on you. Let all your efforts be directed at forging links with Christ. Make the words of John the Baptist your own: "He must increase, but I must decrease."

There have also been developed "Twelve Rules for Caring." They are:

1. Start where people are in need and interest.
2. Be unshockable.
3. Do not be easily rebuffed, yet respect the integrity of every person.

4. Remember: moralizing antagonizes; the gospel of Jesus wins.
5. Never pass on a confidence given.
6. Be available, making clear how you may be reached.
7. Under no circumstance give personal financial assistance.
8. Do not judge people by their cover-up; look always for causes rather than effects.
9. Lead people into fellowship with others, remembering that worship is the greatest therapy of all.
10. Prepare the cared-for to care for others.
11. Love before you try to convert, but point always to Christ as Savior.
12. Remember the words of Jesus: "Without me you can do nothing."

General Service

There are at least five hundred people, in one way or another, linked with Life Line. Some of the tasks which need to be done are quiet, humble, without the drama of telephone counseling and the Caring Division. Without the service of men and women who are ready to serve in simple ways, Life Line could not operate.

Into the Life Line clothing store pours an endless stream of clothing. It must be sorted, washed, ironed, mended, and stacked. On roster are many women who are willing to serve in this way.

We try to preserve the dignity of people who need secondhand clothing by giving a certificate which can be used in the Opportunity Shop attached to the Centre. There also are try-on rooms where every effort is made to find the article of clothing that fits and is suitable.

Life Line operates a number of Opportunity Shops throughout the city. In these, clothing and furniture are sold at cheap prices, offering a service to the poorer segments of the community. It is one way by which Life Line obtains some of its necessary finance to cover the heavy operating costs. Voluntary workers staff these shops, finding in this way another avenue of aiding Life Line.

Life Line has its own grocery store. Many firms make regular gifts of food. From them and the annual Christmas door-to-door appeal for canned food come the supplies which allow food parcels to be prepared to meet emergency food needs. Jesus accurately interpreted human society, for even in a day of affluence his words remain true: "You always have the poor with you."

The Life Line Movement is larger than the Life Line Centre. For all forms of service we encourage people to join the Movement. The Mission Restaurant must be staffed. Adults are needed to assist the running of youth clubs. A group dynamic policy requires many helpers. Hostesses, receptionists, a pool of typists—all find a place in the far-flung work of the Mission.

Out of the ashes of the main auditorium of the Sydney Mission, which was destroyed by fire in 1963, has arisen a great Christian community centre called Wesley Centre. Here operates a Christian club. To the centre come several thousands of people weekly. They are found in its interest groups; they use its eating facilities, its game rooms, its lounges, its library, its chapel.

The General Service Division of the Life Line Movement supplies the team of volunteers that staff Wesley Centre. Here too only trained people are used. The hostesses at the reception tables on the various floors, the restaurant assistants, the people aiding assimilation and offering friendship within the groups have all passed through the training courses designed for the General Service Division.

The basic instruction course under the general title "Serving in the City" includes the following lectures: "The Open House Ministry," "Working Within a Group," "Coping with Difficult People," "Making New Contacts," "Following Up Our Contacts," "Getting People Involved," "Conversion Is the Goal."

It does something to people to become linked to a movement. Isolated service has its satisfactions, but there is added reward in being linked with others in a large task. Through it all we are seeing the result which many a writer has prophesied, the renewal of Christian allegiance through involvement in a direct and personal way in the cause of Christ and the service of people.

Young Life Liners

"I was wandering along a city street wondering what to do," is the testimony of an eighteen-year-old Australian. "Brought up in a children's home, I now had to look after myself.

"Suddenly I heard a band, and stood looking in the door at the Teen-age Cabaret. I had a terrific inferiority complex and did not go in. A week later something drew me back. I went in and stood in a corner. Someone came up to me. I learned later he was on the service team of the Cabaret, a member of the Life Line Caring Division. He introduced me to others, even to members of the band.

"It was a shock to find that the Teen-age Cabaret was run by a church. I didn't think churches did things like that. I became interested. I began to attend the theater service on a Sunday night. I wanted to play my part in what was being done for teen-agers. I decided to become a Christian and I learned what it is to be converted."

This young Australian became a member of the service team. He spent a year in the Evangelists' Institute of the Mission where, for twelve months, young people are trained for Christian leadership.

There is a Young Life Liners Division in the Movement. It is open to all young people who are willing to accept the conditions of membership and are ready to attend lectures. Lectures are held every Sunday at 5:00 P.M. when youth is trained to serve youth.

The Teen-age Cabaret is the outreach program of the Mission. For years it has been operating on a Saturday night. Capacity house—six hundred teenagers—is a regular experience, and often scores or hundreds are unable to gain admission.

The Cabaret begins at 7:00 P.M. and ends at 10:30 P.M. Throughout the night a five-piece band plays and youthful artists sing. At 9:30 P.M. there is the all-important Christian floor show. A fast-rhythm gospel choir sings, and a brief Christian message is given. Following this featured presentation, teen-agers are invited to come and speak of their problems. And they do, as contacts and friendships are developed over the months.

The Teen-age Cabaret is staffed by fifty people every Saturday night. The service team gathers at 6:00 P.M. for a prayer meeting and a briefing session. The key service rendered is in the friendship corps. Throughout the night young people are moving among the packed two floors of the centre, making friends with the teen-agers, seeking to express a Christian concern, hoping to be able to bring others to the knowledge of Christ they have. It forms the chief outlet for service for Young Life Liners.

Out of the hundreds of contacts at the Teen-age Cabaret has developed the youth advisory service of Life Line. Young people are encouraged to call with their boy-girl, parent-child problems. In confusion over sex, in the clashes between authority and freedom, in the moods and fears which arise along the fateful passage between childhood and adulthood, the advisory service is available.

The teen-age years are lonely years. So often parents and teachers are almost the last ones to whom youth turns for guidance. But Life Line? Again the impersonal yet personal telephone and the stranger who can keep a confidence offer guidance.

Standing behind the telephone counselors, the contact people, is the panel of youth advisors. University lecturers, trained youth leaders, social workers, ministers, are available for interviews. Where needed, interviews are arranged for the young people who call.

The Miracle of Money

"Please accept as an Easter offering from a very grateful Christian a check for $2,000. This is just a very slight token of gratitude to God for all he is and always has been to me. After reading of the many fine works your Mission is engaged in for the betterment of our people, I would like to contribute something toward the work."

The writer was an old lady who had watched a telecast of the Easter sunrise service which we hold annually in a Sydney drive-in theater. From a tall platform erected in front of the large white screen the Easter message is preached. The offering on Easter morning is for Life Line. It is one of the ways by which Life Line is financed.

The Life Line Centre cost 100,000 Australian dollars to build. This came almost entirely from the general public. Each year Life Line costs $55,000 to operate. Again, a generous church and generous public supply what is needed. No government subsidy is received. It is in faith that we set out each January, knowing that by December from somewhere another $55,000 must be found.

Sydney has adopted Life Line. Mass media support has achieved this result. A Sydney newspaper, the *Daily Mirror*, sponsors a Life Line Christmas appeal. Each day for a month before Christmas a story of human need is told out of Life Line files, and a daily acknowledgment of gifts received is made. Radio and television stations carry frequent reports of the work. As a result, unsolicited gifts are often made, and a foundation of informed and friendly public opinion for times of special appeal is laid.

The Life Line radio program is broadcast weekly over fifteen stations throughout Australia. A modern band was engaged to record in six different rhythms the old revival hymn, "Throw Out the Life Line." A fast-rhythm version is the signature tune of the program.

The content of the program is the reading and answering of letters written asking for advice. It is virtually a mass counseling session. Hymns in modern rhythm and protest folk songs are used to break the speaking. Always an appeal for financial help for Life Line is made. It is another way by which funds are gathered to maintain the work.

The Holy Spirit knows our needs. He brings the answers. This is the constant miracle we have come to expect here. In amazing ways special demands are met.

Take one example. A new director for Life Line was appointed. With his family he was to arrive from overseas. Somehow a home had to be found for him. Anxiously we faced the demand which it represented on our resources. We began to pray that from somewhere our need would be met.

"I am the executor of a will of a woman who died in Sydney six months ago," was the message which came one day over the telephone. "A house is bequeathed to Life Line. We will be ready within a month to hand it over to you. If you wish to inspect it, you may have the keys."

Wonderingly we set out to a street in a suburb called Botany, only a few miles from the Life Line Centre. We opened the door. The house was fully furnished. A refrigerator stood in the corner, unused linen was stacked in the cupboards, a toaster stood on a bench in the kitchen. The house was completely ready for a family to move in. It had everything.

The Botany house was the first bequest received by the Life Line Centre. When the director, his wife, and two children arrived in Sydney Harbour we were able to take them straight to their new home.

A coincidence or a miracle? I know what we call it. There have been too many incidents which can be described as the "miracle of money" for us to doubt the words of the Bible: "The Lord will provide."

A Service of Dedication

"The Life Line Movement is not primarily an organization, but a spiritual commitment to Christ and his church." This is the essence of the statement on policy which describes the Movement.

The climax of every training course is a service of dedication. Lectures have been attended, interviews completed, a vote of acceptance into the Movement has been taken. There remains dedication.

Life Line demands a long, hard pull. There is excitement, adventure in becoming a telephone counselor, in joining the Caring Division. But what shall remain of a first glad enthusiasm six months, a year, six years, from the day of commitment? Where is there to be found a power to nerve people over the long, often weary sessions of service? This is a crucial issue for every institution, especially those which depend on voluntary service for their maintenance and fulfillment.

Life Line is no exception. It knows from experience the realism of the parable of the sower which Jesus told. There have been those whose lives can be likened to the stony soil on which Jesus said some seed fell from the hand of the sower. "The sower sows the word . . . those who are sown 'on stony soil' are the people who on hearing the word accept it with enthusiasm; but they have no root in themselves, they do not last" (Mark 4:14-17, Moffatt).

The Life Line dedication service calls forth a deep consecration of all who are willing to share in its challenge. Its purpose is to call forth a solemn response, in the presence of the risen Christ, from those ready to make their vows of service. It is designed as a preparation against the day which will inevitably come when, as someone has said, "Our vows rather than our successes must be the source of our inspiration."

The incoming members of the Life Line Movement stand before the Communion rail in Wesley Chapel. Above them is the lighted stained-glass window of Christ with his men around him at the Last Supper. It seems almost that the table is extended and those who today would love and serve him are gathered in the one fellowship.

Each incoming member takes the following vows:

Minister: Are you willing, in dependence on God, to seek to be instruments of his purpose through the Life Line Movement?

Incoming Member: I am.

Minister: Will you hold in confidence all information which may come to you through your Life Line service?

Incoming Member: I will.

Minister: Do you offer yourself for such tasks in the Life Line Movement as are appropriate to your abilities?

Incoming Member: I do.

Minister: As an incoming member of Life Line are you ready to accept the pledge and discipline of the Movement?

Incoming Member: I am.

Then are spoken words of welcome and acceptance:

In the name of the Life Line Movement we welcome you as a full and active member. You are entering into a great service, the service of Christ in his church. Through dependence on Christ you are called to express his compassion to all in any kind of need.

Christ has many services to be rendered through the Life Line Movement. Some are easy, others are difficult; some bring honor, others bring reproach; some are suitable to our natural inclinations and temporal interests, others are contrary to both. In some we may please Christ and please ourselves, in others we cannot please Christ except by denying ourselves. Yet the power to do all these things is assuredly given us in Christ, who strengtheneth us.

4

LIFE LINE DISCOVERIES

Startling Statistics

I am writing during the fourth year of the operation of Life Line. A ministry which began hesitatingly, almost fearfully, has become firmly established. Procedures, modified by experience, have increased in efficiency. A public service has become accepted by the people. Life Line has joined the service scenery of a city.

Statistics are startling. In three years there have been 30,187 people who as first contacts have telephoned, arrived at the Centre unheralded, or written for assistance. Of these, 25,035 have come as telephone calls. Day by day, week by week, the stream flows toward Life Line, the stream of people who, immersed in a great metropolis, reach the point where from someone, something beyond themselves they seek help.

No less significant is the total of 15,377 subsequent face-to-face interviews which have taken place at the Life Line Centre. The majority of these have been handled by the full-time staff of the Centre, but the honorary consultant panels have grappled also unceasingly with human need.

During these three formative years the trouble teams have gone out into potential or actual suicide situations 422 times. No one can estimate how many lives have been saved through the availability of a telephone referral point and the rapid dispatch of a trouble team. At the end of many a week we know in our hearts, without exaggeration, that someone is living whose life would have ended in the tragedy of self-destruction but for Life Line.

The volume of telephone calling is greatly influenced by publicity through press, radio, or television. Only one story has to reach the public through any one of the mass media channels for the number of telephone callers to rise sharply. We have almost reached the stage where we shrink from further publicity, so heavy is the added burden it imposes on an already overstrained centre.

In the year ending March, 1966, the third year of Life Line, statistics tell the story. They show when and where the pressures of need emerge. They allow a profile of the problems of the people of Sydney—and possibly of any large city—to be seen.

During this third year 11,130 counseling contacts were made. Of these, 8,522 came through the telephone: 7,819 being first contact calls, 703 being subsequent telephone calls. There were 2,027 people who came, unheralded and therefore without appointment, to the Centre and were dealt with by what we call "preliminary interviewing"—a telephone-type interview across a table. In addition we received 583 letters asking for help in some form of human predicament.

In this year, subsequent to the first contacts made, 5,551 interviews were conducted at the Life Line Centre. It is in the counseling in greater depth, beyond the telephone, that the most significant happenings are recorded.

In the area of suicide prevention, the third year has been the most significant of all. On 150 occasions it was considered that the threat of suicide was real enough to send speeding through the city the Centre's trouble teams.

An analysis of the calls and interviews shows a profile of the need of a city. The classification of problems uncovers the following picture:

Social Division

Accommodation	1,391
Employment	621
People wanting live-in positions	91
People offering live-in employment	497
Food requests	639
Clothing needs	661
Appeals for financial help	687

Unmarried Mothers and Children's Division
  Unmarried mothers 333
  Adoptions requests 317
  Child care 752
  Family counseling 187
Guidance Division
  Marriage counseling 735
  Domestic problems 491
  General counseling 1,697
  Youth advisory 658
  Legal aid 309
  Pastoral counseling 630
  Miscellaneous 883
Compulsive Problem Division
  Alcoholism 582
  Compulsive gambling 159
  Drug addiction 43
Psychiatric Division
  Psychiatric counseling 840
Suicide Division
  Attempted suicides 105
  Threatened suicides 259
  Potential suicides 87

Out of three years of experience some understanding of when and how times of pressure build up has developed. We have learned in what hours of each day and at what times of each year special demands come. We are beginning to see some correlation between the weather and the ringing of the telephone.

Peak periods on the telephone occur in the late morning, from 11:00 A.M. to 1:00 P.M., and in the evenings from

5:30 P.M. to 11:00 P.M. After midnight relatively few calls are received, but those which do come in the middle of the night are almost always of a very serious type. Many, many times the trouble teams are dispatched after midnight, although a factor operating here is that during the day more people can be encouraged to make their own way to the Life Line Centre.

The weather, of course, seems to have its influence. When rain falls, the calls drop off. Perhaps there is something in the fact that falling rain has a soothing effect on mind and emotions. On dark, cloudy, drizzly days when perhaps increased emotional depression could be expected, calls are reduced rather than increased. Many people go to public phones to call so as not to be overheard by relatives or friends; and after all it is more unpleasant to go out of doors seeking a telephone in the wet!

There is no significant fluctuation over the months from February to October—with the exception of early winter, when a higher demand for clothing and food develops in the Social Work Division.

There are special local circumstances at the Sydney Life Line Centre which explain a sharp rise in telephone calls from November to January. Publicity is greatly increased prior to Christmas because of the Life Line Christmas appeal for funds promoted by the *Daily Mirror*. The appeal brings not only gifts of money and clothing, but increased demands for help.

Christmas, with all its focus on the warmth and joy of the family circle, has a depressing effect on lonely or estranged people. Nevertheless, Christmas Day itself must have some strange comfort of its own to people, for we receive the lowest number of calls in the whole year on December 25. Public holidays as a whole are among the quietest of the year.

So, day and night, the telephone calls come and the knock is heard on the Life Line door. All point to the ocean of distress out there in the metropolis, the unmet need, the urgent need of people in trouble. The breadth and depth of human need in a great city is the most startling discovery of Life Line.

Social Service Division

"You always have the poor with you." As a statement of fact, how right Jesus was. Even in as affluent a society as Australia, pockets of poverty, homes in physical need, and individuals suffering from material distress can all be found.

John was aged forty when he turned to Life Line. It was from The Gap, Sydney's notorious suicide jump, that his first call for assistance came. In deep depression, he believed life was no longer worth living. The trouble team was soon at his side, and later, at the Centre, he unfolded the story of his life.

The child of an alcoholic home, he grew up with violence and instability. His one ambition, as he grew up, was to work with and drive racing cars. Beginning work in a garage, he soon became an assistant on weekends in a racing car pit.

Life then began to go well for him. He married, had

two children, and actually found a garage which was ready to sponsor him as a racing driver. Then, unhappy in his marriage, he began to drink. Turning up at work drunk, shaking hands interfering with his work as a mechanic, he was dismissed.

Now his life began to turn downhill. No one else would sponsor him. His wife left him. Liquor, then methylated spirits, gripped him, and his only home became the parks of Sydney. For a year he had lived this way when he picked up a telephone and called Life Line.

The road back was long and hard. First, he agreed to enter an alcoholic clinic. While he was there, a member of the Caring Division of Life Line visited him constantly. Work was found for him on a country property. Now letters come regularly telling of his love of the country, of his march toward rehabilitation. He is in contact again with his wife. They are corresponding regularly. There is in John's life hope again.

Running through the social work of Life Line are so often the two threads of personal failure and defeat and environmental inadequacy. Their interplay brings destruction to hope and well-being.

Australia is an affluent society, with a per capita income surpassed only by the United States and Canada. In Australia 90 percent have refrigerators and 70 percent possess washing machines. Over 70 percent of the families live in homes which they own or are paying off. A basic wage system provides a minimal living standard to every working man or woman.

There are, however, groups and classes which do not

fully share in the national wealth. There are families, obliged to meet high rental costs for housing, vulnerable to poverty.

Pensioners, numbering 240,000 aged and 47,000 invalids, are not granted adequate pensions. Many live a life of limited activity because of insufficient means; others enter periods of acute economic suffering because of illness or frailty.

The deserted wife often faces want in Australia. She is inadequately protected by law from the consequences of abandonment by the breadwinner, the husband, when left with little children. Many wives will not take the necessary legal action against a husband which would force him to accept responsibility for his children.

To Sydney in recent years have come many hundreds of aborigines. Moving from inland towns and properties they, as so often happens, gravitate toward low-level housing areas and begin to form their own ghettos. In Sydney there is a depressed class of aborigines, and frequently they turn to Life Line.

In addition to poverty and physical distress caused by insufficient income or inadequate housing, there is the material suffering brought on by succumbing to the anti-social forces of liquor and gambling. Self-induced poverty of this kind, bleak and deep, is unfortunately the story of many lives.

Many hundreds of men have reached almost the end of the road in degradation. Living in parks and the various night refuges of the city, almost all show the marks of the excessive drinking of liquor. Some 70 percent of these men, almost unemployable, are in the 35 to 60 age group.

It is a tremendous asset to have, as one agency of the Central Methodist Mission, the Sydney Night Refuge and Men's Hostel. Six cubicles are kept nightly for emergency accommodation needs which may come through Life Line. In addition, dormitory beds are available. Supper, bed, and breakfast are at least better than sleeping in the park.

To meet the human need rising from these causes, personal and social, Life Line carries on its social ministry. It accepts people as they are, and without moralizing seeks to befriend and restore.

Food is given to the family where unemployment, desertion, sickness, death make outside assistance necessary. Clothing is supplied from the clothing store. Limited money is provided for specific needs such as urgently needed medicines and milk for a baby. Accommodation is sought for the homeless, the Mission's Night Refuge being available to the itinerant homeless man. Help in providing a home for an aged relative or a sick or expectant mother is given. Employment is sought for those who, for one reason or another, need an organization like Life Line to open for them the door to employment.

No one can foretell what a day may bring to the Social Work door of the Life Line Centre. It may be the simple, homely request of an old lady for a new home for her pet parakeet now that she must go to an aged persons centre to live. It may be, at the other extreme, assistance which literally is a matter of life and death.

Sometimes Life Line becomes a "lonely hearts club" and an unconscious arranger of romance. On the outskirts of Sydney there lived alone an aging retired man. Needing a housekeeper, he called Life Line. With much care —knowing how difficult it is for some people to find harmony together—a woman pensioner needing a home was suggested. The position was accepted, and nothing was heard from them for months. One day two people, each looking much younger, smiling broadly, called at Life Line. They wanted to thank the Centre's social worker who had brought them together. They were preparing to be married. In gratitude they left a donation at Life Line that the work might go on.

It is through such incidents that Life Line is able to live!

The Unmarried Mother

A taxi pulled up outside our home on the North Shore of Sydney. From it stepped a young girl who asked to see me. For the next hour, in our living room, she unfolded her story.

"I have just come by plane from Western Australia," she began. "You see, I have just learned I am going to have a baby. I don't know what to do. I knew I had to get far away from where people know me. I read in the paper about Life Line. Can you please help me?"

Betty was a Roman Catholic, aged nineteen. She worked in an office and had been going steady with a boy for three months. Then it happened, and there followed the panic flight to Sydney.

We found a home for Betty. While she waited she gave splendid help in all kinds of ways at Life Line. At her request an adoption was arranged for her baby, as soon as that little son, as it proved to be, was born. The day came when again a taxi came to our home. It was Betty to say good-bye and "thank you."

Betty is but one of the endless stream of unmarried mothers-to-be who turn to Life Line in the hour of distress. There has been a steady increase each year, with the third year showing a sharp rise—333 girls, many of them desperate for assistance in emotional crisis.

The illegitimacy rate in Australia has been steadily rising for some time. In 1958 there were 10,131 or 4.79 percent illegitimate births in Australia. The figure for 1965 is 15,531 or 6.89 percent of all births. In New South Wales, for 1965 the number of illegitimate births reached 5,700 or 7.30 percent. And this does not take into consideration those who have illegal abortions; this figure is estimated to be high.

What types of girls find themselves in this dilemma? They come from all levels of society. The large proportion are average Australian youth—attractive, probably having completed three years of secondary school and now employed in a clerical position. Some come from the professions or maybe are training as nurses or students. These girls are not delinquents or libertines who merely live by their instincts. Usually the reverse is the case. The majority of unmarried mothers know little regarding the physiology and true nature of sex. Many have received no accurate sex instruction and certainly have no idea or ideals of Christian love and marriage. Many come from family groups where there has been some degree of fragmentation, such as discord, a broken marriage, or poor relationships. Divorce, drink, gambling, and sexual deviations of the parents are often contributing factors.

The unmarried mother usually comes in a state of conflict and confusion, even despair. Often she is unable to tell her parents. Her friends give contradictory advice. Should she have an abortion? Should she go through with the confinement? Will she keep the baby or surrender him for adoption? And what of her hopes of marriage in the future and her feelings for the father of the baby?

This problem is as ancient as time. In the Old Testament we find Hagar confused and unhappy, a fugitive. Up until the sixteenth century, the community attitudes were reasonable. The girl usually cared for her baby or placed him in a foundling home. Henry VIII, however, despoiled these foundling homes, and the community attitude became harder. The couple was often publicly reprimanded and the father of the child flogged and imprisoned. With our modern enlightened approach—emancipation of woman, freedom of youth, nationally publicized contraceptives—many have failed to give their children a firm foundation for Christian living and a true concept of love and marriage.

What happens after the perplexed girl comes to the Life Line Centre? Immediately we try to allay her fears and give her a brief outline of the facilities available.

Booking for confinement is arranged and appointments are made to attend the outpatients' clinic for regular prenatal care. Accommodation and part-time employment are found. A claim is made for Social Service benefits. Appointments are also made for her to come at regular intervals to Life Line to talk about her problems and plans for the future. Where possible we also try to interview the parents and guide them into a better understanding of their daughter. The father of the baby is often in need of considerable help, and if possible he also is interviewed.

A social history of the unmarried mother and the father of the child is compiled. This will include age, occupation, educational achievements, social interests, physical characteristics, details of parents and siblings, and a full medical history. Personality tests are frequently given, and sometimes arrangements are made for vocational guidance tests. If considered necessary, psychiatric assessment of the girl is arranged with one of our consultant psychiatrists. A Life Line therapy group for unmarried mothers meets regularly, to which all girls are urged to come. Group discussion and training films are used. These groups help to promote free discussion on a wide variety of subjects including ideal marriage and homemaking. Films shown on prenatal exercises and the birth of a baby help to allay fears of the coming confinement.

Legal assistance is given if the girl wishes to take affiliation proceedings and obtain expenses from the father of her child. There is ample opportunity given to discuss the vital question as to whether the girl should keep her child or seek adopting parents. An outline of adoption procedure and the standards required for the selection of adopting parents is given. The legal formalities and implications are fully discussed. Following confinement a Life Line social worker visits the girl several times while she is in the hospital. The baby is also seen and notes are made of physical characteristics and medical history.

The follow-up for some time after confinement is most important. The trauma caused by her emotional conflicts and the confinement leaves almost every girl vulnerable. It is at this time that the compassion and forgiveness of Christ are vital to recovery and to the permanent healing of a moral and emotional wound which otherwise can remain for life. Tenderly, without moralizing, an attempt is made to convey the wonderful message of the New Testament: "Your faith has saved you; go in peace."

Life Line is an adoption agency. It is one of the seven officially accredited adopting agencies of the state and operates under the legislation laid down by the Child Welfare Department of the New South Wales Government. Great care is taken in seeking the right home for a baby or a child when the natural mother desires adoption. Every effort is made to find, from among the three hundred couples a year who approach Life Line for the adoption of a child, the family situation which will surround the child needing a home with love and wisdom. Last year we found homes for sixty babies.

What kind of people apply for the adoption of a child? They come from all levels of society, from the university lecturer to the process worker at the factory bench. Ideally, they will be a typical Australian couple in the process of buying their own home. It will be nicely furnished and have a pleasant garden. This ideal couple will both be members of their local church. Above all, they will have an active faith in God. Even the statistics show that families who attend church together and have faith in God show a far higher rate of marriage stability.

Adopting parents should both be in good health. Medical certificates are required to show that there is no disease past or present which will in any way interfere with their normal life expectancy. The husband should have a good employment history and be well regarded by his employer. They should be financially adequate. This does not necessarily mean they will be in the high income bracket, but rather a couple that has learned to budget wisely and well and live within their income, whether it be $1,800 or $18,000 per annum.

And what of the baby? If the natural mother has appealed to us early enough, then careful preparations can be made for adoption. At confinement and for some days afterward the baby is watched closely for any hint of abnormality. There is examination by the obstetrician and pediatrician, and a rating done which gives a fair indication of normality.

Not all children are adopted at birth. These are the ones for whom it is even more important to make sound decisions, for the child is old enough to react more consciously.

Take, for example, young Judy. If ever a baby needed tender loving care, Judy did. At seven months she weighed only ten pounds. She was pale and weak through under-nourishment. Judy's mother did not care; she fed the baby when she felt like it, and then on a weak and insipid milk mixture. Judy's mother, Joanne, walked into the Life Line Centre and said: "Here's my baby; take her; I can't cope with her any longer. . . ." That was the last we ever heard of the mother.

And Judy? After two or three weeks of special care and diet she went to loving parents. On her first birthday she came to see us again. Now she is a happy, lively child, bright and alert, toddling around, the pride and joy of her new parents.

How and when should children be told of their adoption? Part of the process of interviewing adopting parents includes a full and frank discussion on this difficult topic. Frankness and truth are always recommended.

Life Line advises adopting parents to draw on their biblical and Christian heritage. The story of Moses, so loved by all young children, is an excellent way of introducing the fact of the child's adoption, and even a small child will soon comprehend.

In the Bible story, Jochebed surrenders her baby, Moses, because his whole future depended on this—his safety, his education, his training, and even his life itself. Then along comes the princess and "adopts" this baby as her own. If the child sees his new mother as the princess, the unfolding of the story becomes easier.

Being a parent, whether natural or adopted, is a difficult task. It presents a challenge to create an environment where the child's personality will develop and be enriched.

All children are different whether natural or adopted. Parenthood, like marriage, is for better or worse. If the lines of communication between parent and child are kept open, if the child feels accepted and loved for himself, and if he feels secure, then the scene is set for successful parenthood and happy family life.

A Gateway for Children

"Mummy told me to get out and never come back," said a nine-year-old girl. A truck driver passing a corner of a Sydney suburb had found the child crying bitterly. Picking her up, he brought her to Life Line.

An inquiry showed that the girl's statement was true. Her mother, now living with a *de facto* husband, tired of the child. She wanted nothing more to do with the child of her earlier lawful marriage.

The frequency of the abandoned child in today's Sydney is one of the unexpected discoveries of Life Line. In the first year so often were children literally left on the doorstep of Life Line that we were forced to build a new type of home: an emergency refuge for children, now named "Gateway."

Let me step back for a moment. Life Line has a Division of Child Care. To it are referred all cases of unmarried mothers, child care, adoptions, and specific family counseling. In the third year of Life Line 752 families, with an estimated minimum of 2,000 children, sought help at the Life Line Centre. It would have been impossible for any one organization to have assisted fully so large a number of children. However, all requests for help are investigated and alternative solutions sought, either by referring to another agency or possibly helping families overcome their difficulties in some other way. For example, it sometimes is possible to persuade a relative to help temporarily or to find a housekeeper or live-in position to enable a deserted mother to work and earn enough to feed her family.

It was the volume of need which led us to open Gateway in September, 1964. Gateway is a modern brick building, erected at a cost of approximately $40,000, designed for short-term and emergency care of children from the age of two to sixteen years. In approximately two years since its doors opened, 320 children have been accommodated. The total accommodation provides for fourteen children and the daily average is 13.2!

How do these children come through the open doors of Gateway? The initial request usually comes to the telephone counselor at Life Line. During the day, if it appears to be a crisis situation, the matter is immediately referred to the director, and the child, after investigation, will be admitted. If the crisis arises at night a trouble team may be authorized to go and take the child to Gateway. The social worker follows up the case the next morning. If it is not an emergency situation, two interviews are held before admission. This ensures that other avenues of caring are explored.

What types of children come and why do they come? Mostly the children are bewildered and confused, usually incredibly dirty and hungry, often frightened. Some bear the marks of a mother's or father's violent temper, such as bruises and abrasions.

Late one evening a senior archdeacon of the Church of England phoned to say he had found five children wandering on the steps of St. Andrew's Cathedral in Sydney. Could we help? Immediately the children were brought to the Centre. Necessary particulars were sought as required by the State Child Welfare Department. The mother was found but was too confused and intoxicated to be coherent. The children, whose ages ranged from seven to eleven years, were admitted to Gateway. They were desperately hungry, having had nothing to eat all day. The following morning, outfitted with good clothes and the necessary books, they started school and the first stage of a new way of life.

Many calls are received from hospitals. Sometimes we see the lighter side. For example, a call came from a Sydney hospital. Three children required immediate help. Where was the mother? In the labor ward! Where were the children? Playing in the corridor outside the labor ward!

The reasons for admission to Gateway are many and often complex. The main reasons would seem to be the mother in the hospital for a confinement or illness; the mother or father in the hospital as a psychiatric patient; unsatisfactory home conditions; children abandoned; desertion by the mother, with the father unable to care; desertion by the father, with the mother unable to care; a parent in prison; the mother unmarried. It is a reflection of our society that one out of every three children admitted have one or both parents in a psychiatric hospital. Of the 175 boys and girls who came into our care in one year, 54 had parents married and living together; 70 had parents who had separated; 14 had parents who were living in a *de facto* relationship. Only 4 children had parents who were divorced, but 33 were the children of unmarried mothers.

The Sydney Central Methodist Mission has a long history of service in the field of child care. In three homes the Mission constantly caters for 140 children. Very rarely is there a vacant bed. And the aim is not to fill the beds; rather the reverse! Need today is obviously as great as ever.

An affluent society has failed to alter human personality. In fact, it seems likely that the very affluence is contributing to greed and greater crime. Gambling, alcohol, and the striving for material goods have become more important than spending time with the children at home. Cruelty to children in modern society seems to be increasing. Following are comments made by children admitted to Gateway: "Mummy has left us; she wouldn't make our tea and Daddy is running around with a gun"; "Mummy has taken a whole bottle of tablets and she won't answer"; "If I'm naughty Mummy pushes my face down the toilet."

What therefore is the aim of Life Line and Gateway? It is not merely to give temporary care to children and send them back again after a time to the same environment. When a child is admitted, as much of the family background and history as possible is obtained. A condition of accepting the child, under normal circumstances, is that the parent or parents come at regular intervals for counseling. The aim of our social work is to help each person to a greater degree of self-understanding. The immediate problem presented to us is usually only the result of a much greater and deeper maladjustment and need. The needs are usually threefold: physical, emotional, and spiritual. For this reason it is often necessary to enlist several members of the team: a child guidance officer with play therapy for the child, a marriage counselor for the parents, a psychiatrist, a pediatrician, and a minister. In other words, a team of specialists and consultants is needed to cover the many aspects of human need. It is part of the uniqueness of Life Line that it has in its service such a team.

Guidance for Marriage

One of the most critical struggles in the realm of social conduct and relationships today is the struggle to maintain the integrity and stability of the marriage bond. Probably never before in history has the institution of marriage been assailed from so many sides or undermined with such subtlety.

Life Line, with its readily available counseling service "as close as the telephone," is inevitably drawn right into the thick of the struggle. Every day telephone counselors listen to the stories of disintegrating relationships and tension in the home.

Marriage counseling is a complex and delicate skill. Telephone counselors know that many hours must be spent with each couple if there is to be any hope of marriage reconciliation. The telephone is the point of contact, however, and much depends on that first conversation and how it is handled.

For so many who call there is a deep sense of shame in having to admit to a complete stranger that a marriage has failed. Therefore the step from a telephone conversation to a personal interview with a marriage counselor is a costly one. Gently each is encouraged to see that such a step, even though it be an admission of defeat, can be a move toward an answer.

In the third year of Life Line 735 people contacted us with serious marital problems, and 294 of these responded to the invitation to meet with a marriage counselor. As usual in marriage counseling, it is so often true that only one partner is willing to seek help while the other resists the idea altogether. While it is, of course, far better to be working with both husband and wife, we have found that even if this never comes about, counseling with one party of the marriage over a considerable period can open new doors of understanding and insight and vastly improve the situation.

It is more often than not a wife, in desperation, who makes first contact with us. A husband can escape from his marital problems by throwing himself into his work or spending more and more time with other men at the local club or hotel. His wife, on the other hand, is anchored in the home with the constant knowledge that somehow things have gone wrong, and lives with a growing fear for her children and the future. It is then that the telephone rings at Life Line and a problem is shared, perhaps for the first time.

The most critical period in a home seems to lie between the third and fifth years of marriage. The first flush of married bliss is past; the first children have come, throwing more strain on emotional and financial resources. If there has not been a wise adjustment by each partner in the first two years of marriage, the secret sense of failure and frustration by the third year is no longer easy to hide, and the strain comes out into the open. It is at this point that the very ease with which Life Line can be reached becomes significant. An initial telephone conversation makes it possible for people psychologically to seek help at a deeper level and to move on to full marriage counseling.

Lack of emotional maturity is probably the greatest single causative factor in the marital problems that come to Life Line. With the growing number of early marriages, and because an ever-increasing number of young people are entering marriage without the necessary emotional resources to cope with its demands, immaturity is inevitable. Again and again we hear the confession: "I never knew marriage would mean so great a change in my living; no one told me about the responsibilities it would entail." As a result, marriage counseling is often an essential exercise in the process of growing up.

Because of the unbalanced and distorted emphasis on sex in today's society, thousands of young people go into marriage with little, if any, mature understanding of the role of sex in the marital relationship. In over 80 percent of marriage problems unhealthy sex attitudes or ignorance of the simple facts of anatomy and physiology exist. With tact and understanding an attempt is made to lead young people out of desperate unhappiness into a new perspective on sex and an appreciation of its sacramental value.

A growing number of engaged couples are telephoning Life Line seeking premarital counseling. Here a firm foundation can be given so that marriage can be approached in a responsible way. An understanding of the different emotional needs of man and woman and a sense of realism are imparted, and an attempt is made to show the subtle differences between romantic love and married love. Advice is given about budgeting. Guidance is offered on family planning, usually by Life Line's medical panel. Religious factors play a divisive part in many a marriage. Therefore the importance of reaching an understanding in premarriage days is stressed where a mixed marriage is involved. In these cases the priests or ministers of the different churches are called in, and a discussion free of emotional pressure or prejudice often clears the air. The number of calls requesting premarital counseling shows the need in this field, for prevention is better than a cure.

The help of Life Line is sought at varying stages in the disintegration of a marriage. Tragically, the call often comes when a marriage is already broken almost beyond repair, when long separation has taken place, or when a wife can no longer support herself after desertion by her husband. Sometimes assistance can only be offered in the legal sphere, such as financial aid sought for a deserted wife and her children.

The hidden violence which occurs in countless homes is evidenced by the condition of many women who come, bruised and beaten, to seek physical protection from their husbands. Almost always the vicious influence of alcohol is most brutally felt where it is usually hidden from society, in the home. The seven-year-old child who phoned us at midnight pleading that we come "and stop Daddy beating Mummy" was one of many. Again and again we see the sheer determination and courage of wives who wait each week for the return of their drunken husbands, hoping that enough of the pay-check will be left to pay the bills and feed the children.

Sexual guilt, related to some past indiscretion or premarital experience, cannot be wished away. Guilt and remorse eat into the harmony of marriage; and until the past is faced and forgiven, it remains as a buried cancer in relationships, often making healthy and fulfilling physical unity impossible.

There came to the Centre one day a woman of forty-five, who had been married for twenty-three years. She desperately wanted to play her role as a wife with freedom and self-giving but found that something was holding her back. Careful and gentle probing by the marriage counselor revealed that at the age of eighteen, four years before her marriage, she had become pregnant in a casual relationship, and she was pressed into procuring an abortion. Throughout her married life the guilt of this action had haunted her, strangling her ability to give herself in love. As she sat in one of the counseling rooms at Life Line, twenty-seven years later, she was disclosing her frightening secret for the first time.

In such situations the essentially Christian focus of Life Line is important. To whom can a person weighed down with a burden of guilt go, apart from God? Only forgiveness can heal that kind of wound. Life Line aims to help people to live in harmony with each other through imparting something of the spiritual significance of married love. It emphasizes that in the deepest of all unions between human beings, in marriage, there can be the reflection of fellowship with God, the deepest fellowship of all. At Life Line there is the deep conviction that no person can give himself wholly to another until he himself has found true wholeness of personality, and only Christ can make men truly whole.

He was a business executive. For twelve months his wife had been separated from him, living with another man. Their only son was in a children's home.

Somehow, he said to me, he could not forget her. He had heard she was unhappy. Perhaps there was a chance she would return. Would Life Line please reach her, telling of his readiness to forgive and to receive her back?

"Make your own contact with her," was the advice given. "It will mean more for you to do it. If you fail, we might try."

Two weeks later, by appointment, they came together. Weeks of counseling followed. Then came the climax. One day she shyly opened her purse and drew out her engagement and wedding rings. "Do you think you could put these back on my finger?" she said to her husband.

I thought it was time I left the room to discuss an appointment with my secretary. I closed the door behind me. I made sure they had fifteen minutes together.

"Could you remarry us?" was the question which greeted me when I returned. "Well, no," I said, "you can only be married once. But we have a service for the renewal of marriage vows which we sometimes use."

So it was, two days later, we assembled, the three of us, in Wesley Chapel. Quietly I gave the word of invitation: "We are come together in God's presence to reunite in marriage two who have made their vows of lifelong love and loyalty. We come before God and each other penitently. Sin and failure and selfishness have marked our way. Now we seek a new beginning."

After a prayer and a reading of Paul's great "hymn to love" in the thirteenth chapter of Corinthians (Dr. Moffatt's translation), the moment for a renewal of vows came.

"Will you receive your wife, to live together anew in the holy estate of matrimony? Will you love her, comfort her, honor and keep her; and forsaking all other, keep yourself only unto her, so long as you both shall live?"

"I will," the husband said in a low voice.

"Will you receive your husband, to live together anew in the holy estate of matrimony? Will you love him, comfort him, honor and keep him; and forsaking all other keep yourself only unto him, so long as you both shall live?"

"I will," replied the wife.

And so, two people, renewed in forgiveness and hope, went out into the city street to begin life again, together.

A Psychiatric Ministry

In Australia, as in all highly developed countries with large urban populations, there is a crisis in mental health. One of the frightening phenomena of our time is the ever-increasing incidence of mental illness against which psychiatrists, clinical psychologists, and the psychiatric social workers are waging a losing battle. There just are not enough of them to go around.

Howard Clinebell once said: "There is no realistic hope in the foreseeable future of bridging the vast chasm between the need for helping people and the available professionals." After visiting the Sydney Life Line Centre, Professor Clinebell commented: "Agencies such as Life Line, manned by people whose natural therapeutic personalities have been released and channeled through training, are vital services for bridging the gap."

In the third year of Life Line 840 callers indicated a need for urgent psychiatric help, a number comprising 7.3 percent of the total callers that year. Add to these 582 cases of alcoholism; 43 drug addicts; 451 attempted, threatened, or potential suicides; many of the 333 unmarried mothers; and the severely disturbed parties in some of our marriage counseling encounters, and it is possible to sense how great is the need.

Since the Life Line telephones opened, one of the Centre's great ministries has been to mentally disturbed people and often to their families as well. A call comes near midnight: a distraught mother is pleading with us to go to the aid of her nineteen-year-old son. "He is

107

wandering around King's Cross," she says, "accosting people and insisting that he is the messiah. He may get hurt, or worse still, he may hurt someone—he gets terribly violent when this comes over him."

This mother has never heard of schizophrenia; she only knows that her boy is in need, and that Life Line is for people in need. The trouble team eventually finds him and coaxes him gently into the waiting car to be taken for hospital treatment at one of Sydney's psychiatric admission centres. In this case there is probably no hope of cure, but tender care is secured in the crisis, and in the months that follow that mother is given the supportive friendship of a Life Line carer.

Telephone counselors are trained to be vigilant for signs of psychiatric disturbance. Often a caller who has not been able to summon the courage to seek psychiatric help dials the Life Line number and the counselor persuades that person to come for an interview. Such people usually see the director, who seeks to assess the need for professional treatment. If this is necessary, the friendly and trusting relationship created overcomes moods of dread and resistance. Thus Life Line operates as a vital halfway house for many who might not turn to psychiatric help.

A psychiatrist consults at the Centre once a week, and Life Line has a referral panel of seven of Sydney's leading practitioners in this field. A great resource behind Life Line is the forty-two-bed psychiatric hospital which is operated by the Central Methodist Mission. To this hospital and its psychiatrists many an urgent case is referred.

Often telephone counselors and members of the Caring Division, although not professionally trained, can provide supportive therapy when professional help is not immediately available. Sydney's psychiatrists are among the hardest working men in the city, and their waiting lists are long. An interview with an understanding and caring counselor often eases the waiting time.

Life Line has faced an extraordinary variety of emotional and psychiatric needs. There was, for example, the case of a company director. He had to travel widely, and feared that all he had worked for would collapse around him because he had developed an overpowering fear of air travel. One morning he picked up the telephone at the airport and had a ten-minute talk with our counselor before his aircraft took off. On his return he visited Life Line to tell how a prayer on the telephone that day had sustained him. Then he asked for further professional help to deal with his anxiety state.

Take another case. A young teen-ager, facing her first big examination, suddenly developed paralysis of the right arm. Life Line supplied an amanuensis for the examination. There followed counseling sessions with the centre's child psychologist.

Advanced thinking in the treatment of psychiatric and emotional problems is coming to be more and more appreciative of the role of the group and of the total community in healing. The phrase "therapeutic community" describes a whole new world of treatment for the mentally ill. It is in the context of this new thinking that the Christian focus of Life Line extends its power to heal.

"One of the major causative factors in mental illness is the vast, creeping 'unrelatedness' and depersonalization which seems to go along with increased urbanization," to quote Professor Clinebell again. The church of Jesus possesses a tremendous resource for healing in the power of Christian fellowship. So it is that beyond the professional care provided, Life Line counselors always seek to relate people with emotional problems to Christian fellowship and Christian worship.

Dealing with mentally ill people is not without its risks. Twice, members of the staff have been subjected to fierce assaults from deeply disturbed persons, one of whom was later charged and found guilty of the murder of a small boy. In many instances telephone counselors have been able to coax people who have committed criminal acts into surrendering themselves to the authorities. In following through such cases Life Line's director has at times been able to present evidence insuring that a defendant's state of mind be taken into account in deciding innocence or guilt.

It was on a Sunday afternoon that a call came from one of Sydney's fashionable suburbs. A young wife was on the line: "I'm only twenty," she said, "and I'm expecting our first child in six months. We've just moved into our new home and a few minutes ago the police came and took my husband away." She broke into almost hysterical sobbing: "They say they have arrested him for indecent exposure! I feel sick. I want to die! How could he do a thing like that? What kind of man could do things like that? What can I do?"

Emergency steps were taken to obtain legal representation for the twenty-three-year-old husband when he appeared in court the next morning, and a stay of hearing was obtained. Then over the next four months specialized psychiatric care in one of Sydney's hospitals helped him to understand what lay behind his deviant behavior. He responded well to treatment, only too glad that at last he could speak freely about something that had tormented him over the years. Meanwhile, at Life Line, regular supportive interviews with his young wife enabled her to overcome her repugnance and sense of betrayal, to see her husband's problem for the illness it really was, and to stand by him through the ordeal of the trial. They began to attend worship together, finally linking up with a church in their neighborhood. By the time of the trial they were both prepared, and when the husband was released on a good behavior bond they could face the future, still together. Three months later a radiant couple came to ask Life Line's director to baptize their newborn daughter.

The anonymity of the telephone has encouraged many sexual deviants, burdened by shame and guilt feelings, to take the first step in seeking help. The plight of the homosexual and the lesbian is familiar to Life Line's telephone counselors. Many young people in their teen-age years are distressed by homosexual tendencies in a society which increasingly flaunts deviant behavior and yet offers little true compassion to those who are in its grip. When these young people can be persuaded to come in to the Centre for counseling, many of them benefit from the discovery that they do not fight alone and that they can be helped not only through professional care but through the liberating power of Jesus. Some do learn to make the wonderful journey from the bondage of sensualism to the freedom of Christ.

A mind darkened by mental illness is more deeply in need of the language of Christian love than any other, often because that language is the only one that can penetrate the darkness. Mary is seriously ill. She often telephones us yet has never revealed her full name. As a child her father repeatedly assaulted her and she carries a terrible scar today on her mind. She hates all men and never speaks to them. When she goes to bed she hears her father's voice in the room. She cannot shut out the mocking laughter that seems to press in on every side. It is then that she lifts her telephone somewhere in Sydney and dials Life Line. We know her and have learned how to ease her agony. The conversation always ends with a prayer for peace and quiet sleep. Mary may never summon the courage to come for further help—we hope she will —but now she turns to Life Line, and Life Line is there.

The Compulsive Gambler

Jane telephoned Life Line late one Friday evening. She had been wandering the city streets desperately wanting to talk to someone, until the thought came to her: "Call Life Line." "I do the bookkeeping for our company," she said. "I am well paid and I have a husband and two children whom I love very dearly, but I am an inveterate gambler. Nearly every night I play the slot machines or visit the baccarat games; I just can't stop myself—it's like a fever with me." She went on to tell the listening telephone counselor of how she had used five hundred dollars of the company funds to maintain her gambling: "I've done it before, just to tide me over, but the auditor is coming on Monday and I haven't a hope of paying it back before he discovers it. I want to go to prison; a person like me has to be locked up to be kept away from gambling. But what will become of my family? I will never be able to face them after this!"

Jane was one of more than 150 compulsive gamblers who contact Life Line each year, usually in desperate circumstances. She listened while our telephone counselor told her of others with the same problem who had found hope through joining one of the Gamblers' Liberty Groups that meet weekly at the Centre. As she heard of the road to recovery that had opened out to many of them, she made a decision. Jane decided to telephone her employer there and then to be honest with him about her misuse of funds and the reason why she had done it. She told him that she had at last found someone who seemed to understand her problem; a voice on a telephone had told her for the first time that she was probably a compulsive gambler, a sick person in need of healing, and that she was not alone anymore. She asked him for a chance to try the Gamblers' Liberty Group at Life Line. Because in every other way Jane was an excellent worker, her employer readily agreed, and after an interview with Life Line's director she was introduced into the group.

113

In New South Wales, as in many other places, the gambling industry has reached mammoth proportions. Australians will traditionally bet "on two flies climbing up a wall." Newspapers will devote sometimes as many as five pages to horse racing alone, and everywhere there are lottery shops and legalized off-course betting facilities. The hundreds of returned servicemen's and sporting clubs make the greater proportion of their gigantic profits out of their slot machines, or "one-armed bandits." Illegal baccarat and "two-up schools" flourish in Sydney's King's Cross, scorning the state's betting and gaming laws.

Behind the veneer of glamor and excitement there lies the misery of financial disaster, broken homes, and sometimes even suicide of those who have been unable to control their gambling. In an emotional climate conducive to excessive gambling there are always those who will gamble foolishly or extravagantly, but more tragic still are those who are particularly vulnerable to the compulsive-type addiction. Rather like the alcoholic with his first drink, once they begin to gamble they lose all control and will gamble away every cent they can lay their hands on. The American Mental Health Association estimates that there are six million compulsive gamblers in the United States alone.

"Most people gamble for money," said Rick, a compulsive gambler in his mid-forties, with twenty years of solid betting behind him, "but I worked two jobs for five years just so that I could keep up my gambling, and even then I ended up in prison.

"When my wife and children were with me I got so low

I used to rob the kids' piggy banks at times; most of the stuff in our home was pawned more than once, and when I had a big win I used to buy my wife something valuable —something that would bring back a good price if I needed money in a hurry. When the craze grips me I do things that would make a sane man sick."

Here in a Sydney club is a solitary businessman standing at the poker machine gallery, playing two twenty-cent machines simultaneously. His eyes are glazed and his movements almost automatic. For thirty-five minutes he inserts coins and pulls the handles, one with each hand, pausing only to cash more checks at the bar. In that time he puts an estimated one hundred twenty dollars into those machines, and the returns from both possibly total forty dollars. He walks out with a completely expressionless face. There are thousands like this man in Australia. Such is the power of a compulsion.

Most compulsive gamblers experience agonizing remorse, almost akin to the alcoholic hangover, after heavy losses. They have little memory of what happened while they were gambling and have no desire to remember. The gambler's remorse lasts for a day or two and then begins to wear off. Good intentions and firm resolutions are not enough. He resorts to all sorts of tricks—handing his money to his wife, instructing his club secretary to refuse his checks—all to no avail.

At Life Line it became evident that little or no work had been done in Australia in this field and that a unique program of therapy would have to be devised, structured to cater not only to the basic gambling problem but to related needs as well. Most compulsive gamblers make their initial contact with the Centre because of financial or marital crises that have arisen from their gambling, and they have to be eased into an understanding of the real need, which is to deal with the compulsion itself.

At the heart of the program are the Gamblers' Liberty Groups, where gamblers meet each week under the guidance of Life Line's director and a Christian psychologist skilled in group therapy. Anonymity is preserved by the use of Christian names only. Sometimes the little chapel on Life Line's second floor is crowded with twenty-five people, and on other group nights there have been as few as five, but the group always meets, on the principle that where there is more than one person there is a group.

Wives and husbands of compulsive gamblers are encouraged to participate and so to improve their understanding of the problem that has brought so much suffering and bewilderment to their homes. There are no limits on discussion so long as members remain honest and real with themselves and each other. Together they look for an answer to problems, and so bear each other's burdens along the recovery road. Sometimes discussion is merely supportive; sometimes it cuts hard and deep; always the participants leave with some new discovery about themselves, and renewed hope.

Life Line's existing facilities are utilized to provide help in depth for compulsive gamblers. Marriage guidance is there to help heal broken relationships, and financial guidance to pick up the threads of responsible living. Debts have to be consolidated and realistic payments arranged, while sometimes it is necessary for Life Line to arrange legal representation for those arraigned before the courts on bankruptcy charges. Always there is the twenty-four hour telephone counseling service available for any group member who may find himself alone and unable to fight off his compulsion any longer.

Denis will always remember the day Life Line's trouble team raced to his aid. He had become a regular member of the Liberty Group and had not placed a bet for three months. Then he broke badly and for a week he gambled continuously; he went to the race meetings, the dog races, the trotting meetings—one after another in a feverish round of betting, losing, winning, losing again.

After seven days he awoke from his daze to find himself lying in a shed near one of Sydney's undercover "two-up schools." He had been assaulted by thugs and even his shoes had been taken; he was derelict and he had failed the group. It was then that thoughts of suicide crowded in. He phoned Life Line, and the trouble team found him sitting on the pavement gazing numbly at his bare feet.

Recovery is slow, and there are many setbacks. It is hard for a man to admit that he has been beaten by anything; it is hard for a man to come to see that he may need to attend group meetings for many months. Of the many who telephone Life Line, only 40 percent are willing to take the first step of coming to the group, and even when they do they often come looking for some "miracle

117

cure" or they refuse to accept the group's first principle: "I recognize that I am a compulsive gambler and can never afford to lay another bet."

The roots of the gambling compulsion are many: the immaturity of believing that the world owes a living to its population, escapism from today's faceless society or from domestic responsibilities, the desire to boost one's ego by beating the odds. These and others are discussed and faced repeatedly by the group, but above all, some of the group have come to see that complete recovery will only come with the help of a "power beyond themselves."

On the table in Life Line's chapel stands a small cross symbolizing the Christian focus of all we attempt. Over the group's first twelve months that cross has had its way with a number of members. Sometimes they come alone to seek an interview with the director, who is a Christian minister; sometimes there is just a passing mention of "having gone to church last Sunday." Perhaps the most significant development lies in the request by four members that a supplementary group be formed for the specific purpose of discussing how to know God and use his power through prayer and the Bible.

When Bill came to the Gamblers' Liberty Group he was an agnostic. In discussion he strongly resisted anything remotely "religious" and insisted that God had nothing to do with gambling. Twelve long months later Bill was entering into a spiritual awakening.

"It's nearly six months since I placed my last bet," he said. "The fellowship of this group has done this for me, and now I'm looking for something more than just stopping

118

gambling. The group has made me humble, and when you're humble you begin to realize your need for outside help. I hadn't been in a church for forty years—not since Sunday school. I still haven't gone that far; but the other night I dusted off my mother's Bible, which I have never opened before, and sat down and read the Sermon on the Mount. I think I'm about ready to take up where Sunday school left off!"

Suicide in Sydney

Life Line is much more than a suicide prevention centre, but for Sydney it fills this vital role. Surrounding the suicide call develop the most urgent and dramatic elements of the Centre. So significant has suicide prevention become that, if for no other reason, Life Line justifies all the sacrifice and cost of its operation.

Suicide has become a vast world problem. It is estimated that as many as 250,000 people around the world kill themselves each year. The World Health Organization states: "West Berlin, East Germany, Hungary, Austria, Finland, Switzerland, Japan, Denmark—in descending order—report the highest suicide rates for 1951-59. The lowest rates are in Italy, Spain, Ireland, Northern Ireland, the non-white population of the United States, Colombia and Costa Rica."

Actual deaths by suicide, together with the number per 100,000 of population, are given by United Nations for the year 1964 in the following nations:

No. of Deaths Per 100,000 of Population

West Berlin	915	41.7
Hungary	2,890	28.6
Austria	1,645	22.8
France	7,207	14.9
Japan	14,458	14.9
Australia	1,620	14.5
England and Wales	5,566	11.7
United States	20,588	10.8
Italy	2,709	5.3
Spain	1,532	4.9

There have been several surveys taken on the circumstances surrounding suicide, such as the one by the Mental Health Research Fund in England. While facts vary to some degree from place to place, the following facts about suicide have emerged. The self-destructive impulse is three to four times stronger in men than women. As many as 70 percent of the people who commit suicide give some warning, especially to relatives and friends, that they are intending to do it. The idea that people who talk about suicide do not do it is shown by investigation to be false. Alcohol is a contributing factor in many cases of suicide. Suicide rates have been rising slowly since 1870, apart from the drops which occurred during the two world wars.

A very vital fact is that 65 percent of the people who attempt to take their lives do not, if saved, attempt self-destruction again. In other words, if the crisis of despair which causes the suicide attempt can be negotiated, things apparently do not again reach the same intensity. It is this fact which makes so essential the existence of a known and easily available suicide prevention centre in every city.

The estimates vary concerning the rate of unsuccessful suicide attempts to those that succeed. It is virtually impossible to arrive at an accurate figure because of such factors as the "hidden suicides" cloaked, for example, in road fatalities. However, many would claim that as many as eight people try to destroy themselves for every one that succeeds.

The facts disclose that behind the world suicide story are mountains of unhappiness and oceans of despair. So large has the problem become that it is clear that in many countries and cities adequate preventive, remedial planning and action have scarcely begun.

Suicide rates in Australia are high, and rising. In 1960, 1,092 or 106 per million of population committed suicide. By 1965 it has risen to 1,684 or 149 per million of population. This, of course, represents an increase of over 40 percent in five years.

In Sydney the figures from 1960 are as follows:

$$1960 \ .. \ 232$$
$$1961 \ .. \ 306$$
$$1962 \ .. \ 362$$
$$1963 \ .. \ 468$$
$$1964 \ .. \ 429$$
$$1965 \ .. \ 502$$

Every day of the year an average of 1.4 people in Sydney die by their own hands. If the 8 to 1 ratio between those who try and those who succeed in self-destruction is accepted, then in Sydney someone tries to commit suicide almost every two hours.

During the period from March, 1965, to March, 1966, Life Line received, as we have seen, a total of 451 suicide calls, made up of 105 cases where attempts were actually made, 259 were threatened, and 87 were regarded as potential suicide cases. During this period the trouble team was dispatched 150 times.

An investigation of the suicide cases dealt with by the Sydney Life Line Centre over the third year of its operation disclosed these facts:

60 percent were men, 40 percent were women

30 percent were between the ages of 20 to 29

33 percent were between the ages of 40 to 49

50 percent claimed never before to have attempted suicide

In a detailed analysis of telephone counselors' reports and facts gained in follow-through treatment there emerged a picture of the human situations which lead to suicide attempts:

Marital troubles	27 percent
Alcoholism	20 percent
Loneliness	15 percent
Acute psychiatric disorders	15 percent
Financial difficulties	10 percent
Unmarried mothers	4 percent
Drug addiction	3 percent
Physical sickness	2 percent
Homosexual problems	2 percent
Uncertain causes	2 percent

We have learned to expect two recurrent factors in many suicides and suicide attempts. They are loneliness and the sense of being caught in an impasse, with no other way out seeming to be available save death.

In Sydney suicide is attempted, on a percentage basis, by the following means:

Overdose of sedatives or drugs ....43 percent
Leap from high places ....24 percent
Use of sharp instrument ....12 percent
Other (gas, drowning, poison) ....21 percent

Suicide calls come from all over the city. As in other cities, Sydney shows that inner-city areas, especially where there is a high incidence of living alone, reveal larger numbers of cases than in suburbs where family life is more stable. There is also a wide scatter in the occupations of those turning toward the darkness of self-destruction.

There is one tremendous truth which emerges from three years of experience at Life Line. It is that there does arise a life wish amid the death wish. This is seen in the frequency with which people will call after taking over-doses of poison or turning on the gas jets or slashing their wrists. It is this fact which makes Life Line as a known referral centre an essential community agency.

The Sydney police rang Life Line in September, 1966, to thank its director for the saving of a man's life. This is how it happened.

A forty-year-old man called Life Line one night saying that he had taken an overdose of tablets, and asking that a last message be conveyed to his estranged wife. As the telephone counselor desperately tried to get his address from him, his voice became low and confused. Then there was silence.

A fortunate recollection by the director of an earlier contact made with Life Line led to the discovery of his address. At high speed the trouble team rushed to the possible location. The house was locked; there was no response to knocking. Since they lacked the authority to break in, the police were called. The man was found unconscious by the telephone.

Ambulance, emergency treatment at the nearest hospital, psychiatric treatment, friendship offered through the Caring Division—and recovery.

Then came the word of commendation from the police department: "The hospital tells us that in another thirty minutes it would have been too late!"

What steps should society be taking in the face of the tragic world problem of suicide? All must begin with a new mental attitude, a new concern and compassion toward people suffering from suicidal despair. Attempted suicide is still a crime on the statute books of many communities, such as in the state of New South Wales in Australia, although amending legislation has been promised. The Church of England Prayer Book in Australia denies the use of a Christian burial service for a suicide.

A suicide prevention program would include stricter governmental control of tablets and drugs capable of killing by an overdose. The erection of a sign at a cliff or bridge from which people jump to their death, telling of a place to obtain help, would save lives. Such a sign is erected at Niagara Falls and should stand at Sydney's notorious suicide point, The Gap.

Life Line almost succeeded in having a sign erected at Sydney's Gap. The local council approved of the erection and the wording of the sign. It would have said simply: "There is always somebody who cares at Life Line. If you are in any kind of trouble call Life Line, now. Phone 31 0971. Help is as close as the telephone." Unfortunately, fearing a sign might encourage rather than deter suicide attempts a later council meeting rescinded the permission that had been granted.

There is need for education of the public concerning suicide threats. If as many as 70 percent give warnings of intentions, then the community should be encouraged to take suicide talk from anyone seriously.

Above all, every centre of population needs a well-publicized twenty-four-hours-a-day telephone centre to which the lonely and despairing may turn. Behind it is required an emergency trouble team type of organization, together with psychiatric and other resources to assist in the solving of human problems and the rehabilitation of people.

Suicide, on the deepest level, represents a breakdown of the philosophy of life and of the basic meaning and purpose of living. It also reveals a loss of faith in the worth of human personality. In other words, it touches closely on the deepest of religious issues, the ultimate significance of life and death.

The Christian faith does give answers to the hopelessness and despair which lead to suicide. At Life Line an attempt has been made to express these answers and, in the dramatic grappling with someone over the phone and in the rehabilitation period, to offer the personal garrisoning of life which faith in God can bring.

I know of the impact made on one would-be suicide by one of the Centre's Christian psychiatrists who said to him quietly: "There is no need for you to die; Christ has already died for you." This same man would plead with those referred to him: "Don't think again of taking your life—give it to God and see what he can do with it."

In his book *Suicide and the Soul* James Hillman says: "Suicide prevention for sociology means group reinforcement." [1] This we have learned. With loneliness, the sense that no one cares, an ingredient of many a mood which leads to thoughts of suicide, group fellowship is needed. This Life Line tries to offer through the many groups which operate within the Central Methodist Mission. To rediscover the power of Christian fellowship through worship and the sacraments can be a liberating, renewing experience.

James Hillman claims that suicide is sometimes not an act of despair but an act of hope. He says: "There is an attempt to achieve another state of being through suicide. There is an attempt at transformation. . . . The impulse to death need not be conceived as an anti-life movement; it may be a demand for an encounter with absolute reality, *a demand for a fuller life through the death experience.*" [2]

[1] Hillman, *Suicide and the Soul* (New York: Harper & Row, 1964), p. 26.
[2] *Ibid.*, pp. 71, 63.

The Christian promise that life can be transformed through faith in Jesus Christ becomes in this kind of human situation a relevant word. Conversion, through the death of self and trust in the love and forgiveness of God, can be presented as a reality. In long-term rehabilitation, the aim of which is to see that the dark thoughts of suicide do not recur, the giving of a faith to live by, the offering of the transformation of life which is available here and now, can be and is the answer.

A Faith for Living

Many of the people of Sydney have no link with the Christian church. Some of them are now two or three generations separated from a living religious faith. They have no personal or family Christian memories anymore. They cannot be said to have lost contact with God, for they have never known him. They form that company of people around the world to whom God seems to be dead.

However, one fact is undeniable. The human needs which faith in God once supplied remain in every life. Questions about life, its meaning and purpose, will not be denied. In the end, to every man and every woman comes the human experience of moral guilt, sickness, and bereavement. Then, in that moment, to whom, to what, shall people turn?

Well, in Sydney there is always Life Line. And many, with half-formed spiritual desires, shyly, hesitatingly call a centre which they know is in some way Christian in origin and nature.

A true pastoral ministry, over the telephone or in the counseling situations which follow, is often given. No attempt is made to thrust religious truth on anyone. On the other hand, it is recognized that there is no answer to many human situations unless a life is placed in the context of the spiritual and the eternal. There comes the moment when the initiative must be taken and it is necessary, in New Testament terms, to name the Name of Jesus.

"I would like to talk to a minister," was the first sentence of a woman who called. An interview was arranged, and within a few days she came, telling her story.

"I want to tell you something," she said. "Something nobody else knows. During the First World War my husband went overseas as soon as we were married. After he left I was terribly lonely and linked up with another man, and we began living together. I still wrote to my husband. He knew nothing about it.

"Then my husband was killed in action. The way was then open and we married. Now my second husband is dead."

At this point she opened her coat and showed the war ribbons of her first husband pinned to her dress. "I wear them often," she said. "I cannot forget the wrong I did to him. Do you think I can be forgiven?"

I had noticed her left arm was hanging limply at her side. "You see, my arm has become paralyzed. The doctor says there is nothing to explain it. Do you think it could be caused by what I have done?"

There followed the wonderful privilege of conveying

the message of the forgiveness of God. Gradually she seemed to grasp it intellectually. Then came the acceptance of pardon spiritually, as an act of faith. There was a new look on her face as, after prayer, she left the room. Some days later she phoned to say strength was returning to her paralyzed arm!

Guilt is one of the spiritual situations which drive people to call Life Line. Doubt, intellectual problems about the fact of God, about the Bible, about Christian doctrines cause others to seek help. The sense of the absence of God and the inability to pray form the basis of the spiritual problems of others.

By far the largest number of people with spiritual needs who telephone Life Line are those facing some personal crisis. Sickness, loneliness, bereavement—human situations in which people discover their own weakness—drive them to Life Line.

It is incredible how far many people are from the Christian church. Ignorant of what to do to make contact with the church, embittered because of some failure by the church in their lives—the local minister and church seem to be the last place to which people turn.

It is sad to realize how far the church is from the people. All too often a story is told of the insensitiveness of the church to the real needs of many people. The memory of some moment of blindness or heartlessness cuts deep. So, as an institution, the church is passed by.

There is one fact which emerges clearly out of three years of experience. Religious problems and desires are not far below the surface in many lives. This is shown

129

by how often God is introduced into a conversation, not by the telephone counselor, but by the person at the other end of the line.

A principle can be expressed in this way. When sharing intimacy in a counseling situation it is very easy and natural for the fact of God to be introduced into a conversation. It happens naturally, without strain. Conversation very simply opens out into a discussion about God. There is no resentment; rather, I think there is a hope, a desire that somehow the living God will be encountered. Indeed, it is often that the name of God in such conversations is introduced by the one who has called.

There is often a high moment in the telephone counseling room. It usually comes at the end of a conversation when it becomes right for a prayer to be offered over the telephone. In a surprising number of cases a request for prayer is made, or perhaps a skillful counselor leads up to it. Then heads are bowed, and the ancient miracle of the power of prayer in making people aware of God is repeated.

Many times the counseling room becomes the place of prayer. It is where a man or a woman discovers God. Then it is that another learns the truth of the words of Dr. Leonard Griffith: "God has let down a very long rope that reaches from heaven to the lowest depths of our sin and misery. So I cling to that rope with both hands, and God help me if I ever let go."

Discoveries About God

Many, many are the discoveries which have come through Life Line. There has been an uncovering of the sin and sorrow of a great city. We have seen the range and depth of dedication of which people are capable in neighborly service. Above all we have discovered where and how God works in the lives of people.

God is no detached abstraction. This is the truth which is dawning afresh upon the Christian church today. The God of logic, of a theology separate from life, of religion in separation from life, is indeed a dead God.

But a God involved in the human struggle, a factor in history, a part of time, is very much alive. This is the discovery of Life Line. In new and startling ways, when with such faith and strength as we have we plunge into human need, we find God there.

It is strange how we forget. Jesus came to prove once and for all that God belongs to the world, God belongs to the people. He showed men and women that God was just where they were. His place was among them, just where they lived and worked and laughed and loved. Jesus came to make religion central, real, relevant, vital.

We have, in practice, discovered that we do not take God out into his world. He is there, calling us to join him. He is previous in the lives of men and women to anything we may do. A telephone counselor may have the opportunity to lift up a life consciously into awareness of God, but only because God himself has already been at work in the mind and conscience of that one who has turned to Life Line in a moment of personal need.

There is a deep mystery about many of the telephone calls which come to Life Line. The people themselves often cannot tell why they have reached for a telephone.

I can only explain what happens in terms of the work of the Holy Spirit. It is, I believe, the Holy Spirit who prompts the action.

After all, this is part of the promised ministry of the Holy Spirit. Jesus said before his crucifixion that when the Holy Spirit came he would "bring to your remembrance all that I have said to you." Jesus also said: "When he comes, he will convince the world of sin and of righteousness and of judgment."

A call came one night from a man who said he was phoning from the northern side of the Sydney Harbour Bridge. Emotionally distressed almost to the point of incoherence, he said he had just attempted to throw himself from the bridge into the water far below.

The trouble team which was soon at his side learned his story. Hopelessly involved in gambling debts, unable to tell or face his wife, he saw but one way out. He was actually climbing the protective wire of the bridge when a voice seemed to speak to him: "Call Life Line . . . call Life Line."

Stepping back he found a phone box but could not find the number. Again he climbed the railing, only to be arrested again with the words: "Call Life Line." This time he found the number.

I remember asking him how he had come to seek aid. "I don't know," he said. "I can only remember hearing of Life Line once. It was on a television news program when it opened. I don't know why I thought of it at that moment."

There was another caller, this time from King's Cross.

"I feel rather silly," he said. "I'm acting purely on a hunch. A fellow, looking pretty upset, just asked me where the bus left for Watson's Bay. I told him, and then thought, that's where The Gap is. I wonder could he be thinking of suicide?"

We decided to act. The trouble team which went out found him on the edge of the precipice. He was a young schoolteacher, just jilted by the one he hoped to marry.

This story had a happy ending. For the day came some weeks later when a Sydney newspaper carried the story of an engagement party which showed that at least one lovers' quarrel was not permanent!

Why did the man on the bridge suddenly think, "Life Line"? Why did a stranger, acting on a hunch, enable a man to be drawn back from death to sanity and love? What explanation do you give? I see it all as the working of the Holy Spirit. I make bold to claim that it is indeed the Spirit of God who tells many a man and a woman to call Life Line.

I am not suggesting that if a person has at no time heard of Life Line, God can place that knowledge in the mind. I am claiming, however, that if, even in the slightest way, the fact of the existence of Life Line has been established in the consciousness, the Spirit of God can bring that knowledge to mind at the moment of need. This is the function of the Holy Spirit as described by Jesus. It is the Spirit who is able to bring all things to remembrance.

In the Bible the promise is made, and kept, that the Spirit of God will give wisdom when an answer must be found. In the eighty-first psalm is the promise: "Open your mouth wide, and I will fill it." In Luke, Jesus, speaking of testimonies which must be given before hostile courts, says: "Settle . . . in your minds not to meditate beforehand how to answer; for I will give you a mouth and wisdom." When Stephen faced his antagonists, the book of Acts vindicates the promise of Jesus. It says of Stephen: "They could not withstand the wisdom and the Spirit with which he spoke" (6:10).

In the telephone counseling room at Life Line the reality of this promise is proved again and again. There is so often the feeling of inadequacy, of utter incompetence and helplessness. Who can be sufficient for the situation which unfolds the tragedies of human error and evil? Then, seemingly from nowhere, comes the word which later proves to be the key which unlocked the way to a far deeper level of self-knowledge or to a hidden passage which led beyond an impasse.

From whence comes that word? In humility and wonder the counselor says: It was God.

It is above all in God's dealings with people after they have begun to respond to him that his love and his power are seen. The telephone call, the subsequent interview, the ongoing friendship relationship, group therapy, worship can all be the opening of a life to the transforming presence of God.

Faith in conversion, the transformation of life, either gradually or suddenly, which Christ can bring about is at the base of the thinking of Life Line.

There is something which goes beyond what secular

counseling and psychiatric techniques may achieve. There is something more available than human caring and concern. There is an acceptance to be found which goes deeper than the weaving of an individual into a supportive group.

That something is the removal of guilt and remorse through receiving the forgiveness of God. That something is realizing the love of God. That something is, to quote Paul Tillich's great phrase, to "accept our acceptance" by God himself.

To enter into a new, reconciled relationship with God is to find released into one's personality a healing, binding power which makes men and women whole. At Life Line we work, pray, and expect to see conversion, conversion to God in Christ.

We shall call him John. An illegitimate child, he grew to adolescence in a children's home, knowing nothing of a parent's affection. Before the age of eighteen he spent many months in a reformatory in Victoria. Here was the typical background which so often leads to antisocial and criminal acts.

Then John soon began to show the all-too-familiar characteristics. Journeying to Queensland, he was soon in jail, convicted of stealing. On release he followed the same pattern in New South Wales—finding a door-to-door selling job, he robbed many schools and convents, accepting money for books never delivered.

Forced to leave the state, he began to face the realities of his life in South Australia. He bought a knife, and tells of his struggle to use it to commit suicide on the

135

Glenelg Beach. Lacking the courage, he went to a telephone box intending to give himself up to the police.
Suddenly in the telephone directory he saw the Adelaide
Life Line number. He remembered reading a news story
of the opening of the Sydney Centre.

So it was Life Line, rather than the police, that entered
John's life. Under the friendship and the Christian guidance found at the Adelaide Centre he went straight for
twelve months.

There followed the worst collapse of all. He stole from
the Adelaide church and people who had befriended him.
Again he ran, but not for long. Under the influence of a
friend he returned to Adelaide, confessing his wrongdoing,
expecting again to go to jail.

In Adelaide all John found was forgiveness and acceptance. The moment for climax, for conversion, had come.

"It was one night as I was leaving by train that the
wonder of God's love swept over me. A Life Line counselor
had come to the train to bid me farewell. He actually
put his arm around me as he said good-bye.

"Then it happened. Through that simple act I suddenly
realized the full power of the love of God. I felt washed,
cleansed. I knew that God loved me as a unique person.
He wanted me no matter what I was like. Now I knew I
need run no more."

A new word became part of John's vocabulary, the
word "restitution." As I write he is back in Sydney,
serving through the Life Line Centre as he pays back
week by week a sum of money which will compensate the
convents and schools he robbed. He speaks much of the

rich purpose that now surrounds his life, and of his growth toward maturity.

John now knows, without a shadow of doubt, what he must do. He is preparing to offer himself as a candidate for the Christian ministry in the Methodist Church of Australasia.

5

THE FUTURE OF LIFE LINE

Life Line Goes International

There was a buzz of animated conversation in the foyer of the new two-million-dollar Wesley Centre in Sydney. It was a Friday night in August, 1966. Around the registration table and inquiry desk people were arriving constantly, seeking information, enrolling, gathering name tags and brochures.

The occasion? It was the first Life Line International Convention, sponsored by the Sydney Centre. Over three hundred delegates had registered for a five-day conference.

With a notable panel of Australian and overseas speakers, the convention aimed to grapple with the central human problems thrown up by Life Line experience. It also set out to strengthen links between existent Life Line centres and to plan future action.

By March, 1966, just three years after the opening of the first centre in Sydney, there were sixteen known Life Line centres operating in seven countries. This amazing growth was unanticipated and unplanned. Perhaps the chief cause of the growth was an article in *Time* magazine. From the story presented there, inquiries flowed into Sydney from all over the world. The information sent of procedures and purposes at the Sydney Centre stimulated thought and action, and led to the setting up of centres in other Australian states and beyond.

With the spread of the movement, problems began to emerge. A name, a great name, needed protection so that it might as far as possible be preserved to describe a unique form of service. Standards required formulation and application to present and future centres. Training courses needed examination and confirmation. Intercentre relationships called for examination and development. The time had come for active promotion of Life Line as a creative social-religious form of service in modern society.

As the convention proceeded, a strange change of direction occurred. The planners of the sessions imagined that the chief interest of delegates would lie in the lectures and discussions dealing with personal and social problems. However, it was the business and plenary sessions concerned with the future of Life Line which excited the delegates and became the chief concern of the convention.

"That Life Line International be established by this founding convention": this was the historic decision reached unanimously at the plenary session of the convention in Sydney on Tuesday, August 23, 1966. Only time will tell how historic that decision will prove to be.

The chairman, commenting on the establishment of Life Line International, said: "This is a great day for Life Line. An Australian experiment goes international. In three and a half years, without any specific promotion, sixteen Life Line centres have been set up in seven countries, all patterned on the Sydney Centre.

"Recent happenings like the assassination of President Kennedy, the slaughter of eight nurses in Chicago, the shooting of university students in Texas, focus the need for greater services aimed at grappling with mental and emotional disorders. The coming into being of Life Line centres utilizing trained lay volunteers and professional counseling resources greatly increases the community's capacity for meeting human need."

Following the crucial decision to establish an international organization, a secretariat was appointed. Accreditation was then given to the Australian Life Line centres in Sydney, Adelaide, Brisbane, Broken Hill, and Newcastle, and to centres in Christchurch and Auckland in New Zealand and Stockton (California) in America.

The aims and objectives of Life Line International are:

1. To promote the establishment throughout the world of Christian counseling centres to respond to human need,

based on the telephone staffed twenty-four hours a day by trained counselors.

2. To establish and maintain a secretariat to determine standards for Life Line personnel and procedures.

3. To be the body with ultimate authority and responsibility for the accreditation of Life Line centres and to which each accredited centre is affiliated.

4. To be the liaison body coordinating the policy and work of all Life Line centres.

5. To foster the growth of a Life Line Movement as a body for Christian lay service within the community, emphasizing the importance of discipline and training.

6. To register and protect the names "Life Line International" and "Life Line Centre" and "Life Line" and other derivatives of such names both internationally and nationally.

7. To seek financial support from individuals and foundations and to give financial support to accredited Life Line centres.

8. To arrange an International Life Line Convention not less than once every three years.

What is the future of Life Line? Who knows? Life Line is obviously one of the expressions of a concept of meeting human need which has emerged in different forms throughout the world.

In England and Europe there has developed, under the leadership of the Rev. Chad Varah, the Samaritans. As would be expected in two movements which developed without any knowledge of each other's existence, there are marked differences between Life Line and the Samaritans. Life Line tries to aid people who suffer from any form of

141

distress; the Samaritans began as a suicide prevention centre and continues to focus mainly on the problem of suicide. Life Line is frankly and determinedly Christian in basis and purpose; the Samaritans, while Christian in inspiration and in much of the leadership, seem reluctant to place their ministry in any open religious context. Life Line has at its heart the discipline and strength of the Life Line Movement; the Samaritans have no emphasis on the use of the Christian laity as such, linking their helpers to their work in markedly different ways.

One fact is sure—the Spirit of God is working in new ways through the world in our time. Because we are sure that Life Line International is part of that wide movement of the Holy Spirit, why, in the days ahead, anything can happen!

The Struggle for Standards

The ongoing struggle of Life Line is a struggle for standards. At every level, from the point of contact with the telephone counselors to the professional referrals and aftercare through the Caring Division, standards of training and response must rise.

There is a great peril in the Life Line idea. It is that centres may become established easily and cheaply. Should this happen, failure is certain.

The launching of any Life Line centre demands long preparation, the prior training of volunteers, the gathering of adequate material resources, and the mobilizing of professional panels for counseling and treatment. Without adequate planning, people in grievous trouble can be sadly disillusioned and the whole community disappointed and deceived.

With the perils of shallowness and inadequate planning in mind, Life Line International has set out to establish the highest possible standards of the work wherever it may appear. The Sydney Convention adopted the following resolution:

Basic Requirements of Applicants
 (a) A declared commitment to the Christian faith expressed by active association with the Christian church.
 (b) Personal maturity, and ability to assimilate such training as may be prescribed.
 (c) Acceptance of the discipline laid down by Life Line International and the centre concerned in respect to training and service.

(Credentials relating to the above may be required, including a reference from a minister. The family situation of the applicant, particularly the attitude of the husband or wife, should be taken into consideration.)

Training
The purpose of training is:
 (a) to provide for the spiritual nurture of the applicant, and growth in self-understanding;
 (b) to give knowledge of the spiritual resources available to meet the deepest needs of men and women;
 (c) to present a basic understanding of human personality with its physical, emotional, social, and spiritual needs and attendant problems;

(d) to give knowledge of the art of counseling and caring for people in time of stress;

(e) to give telephone counselors a clear understanding of the limits of their role and of the point at which they should refer situations in accordance with local procedures;

(f) to give telephone counselors an understanding of the special techniques of telephone counseling, and Caring Division members training in the art of home visitation.

Training should include lectures by specialists in different fields, group discussion, role-playing practice counseling, and a period of probation under supervision.

Assessment

The applicant's assimilation of the content of the training program should be tested by such means as a supervised handling of an actual telephone case, use of broken interviews to be completed by the applicant, and an interview by a panel, including, where possible, a minister and an experienced counselor. Before final selection there should be a period of probation on actual service as a counselor. Final acceptance should be followed by an act of dedication including a pledge of loyalty to the movement and confidentiality.

How shall standards be conserved and heightened? There are three ways by which this end shall be reached.

First, no telephone centre should be opened until a trained pool of people is available and preliminary planning has reached an advanced stage. Already in some cities people have imagined that all that is necessary is to find a room with a telephone in it, have a few people who offer to help, and announce to the community: "Help is as close as the telephone."

Nothing is farther from the truth. Almost five years elapsed in Sydney from the first glimmering of the idea of a twenty-four-hour-a-day telephone ministry until the day when the people of an entire city were invited to call. During the last year of these five years, preparation was intense. Money had to be raised, buildings planned, lay volunteers recruited and trained. It was this intensive preparation which alone made possible the acceptance of responsibility and the coping with the volume of work which the opening of the telephone lines brought.

From the experience of existing centres a plea goes forth. Let no one dare to launch Life Line anywhere without the discipline of preparation. To do so is to make failure almost certain.

Second, standards can only be established through adequate training courses. Three disciplines of study must be covered. A basis must be laid in an understanding of Christian doctrine and biblical knowledge. Insight into the environmental pressures which crush in upon people is necessary. Hence, some awareness of the principles of sociology is essential. Human psychology and the nature of the major human predicaments into which people are drawn are proper subjects of study.

A never-ending task is to inspire members of the Life Line Movement to go on growing in insight and knowledge. Refresher courses, conventions, weekend conferences must be offered constantly to telephone counselors and all who dare relate themselves in service to people. All who are unwilling to accept the discipline of growth surely disqualify themselves from the privilege of serving in Life Line.

Third, line after line of resources must be fashioned if answers in depth to human need are to be available. Every telephone contact potentially requires face-to-face counseling by professionally trained personnel and follow-through care and friendship. It is better not to start than to be unable to remain beside someone in need until that need is resolved or recedes.

Finally, the maintenance and lifting of spiritual standards is all-important. The quality of compassion, sensitivity to the leading of the Spirit of God, must not decline if Life Line is truly to fulfill its purpose.

How do we stop from becoming blasé about human need and complacent, unmoved by human tragedy? Telephone counselors at first are overwhelmed by the human scene as it is unfolded on the telephone. A first suicide case is usually almost emotionally overwhelming. But what is the reaction to the tenth and the twentieth telephone call which is probably a matter of life and death? How easy it is to take it all for granted!

To live near to God, to contemplate Christ's respect for people, to be inspired by his compassion is to have human relationships renewed and strengthened. From the love of God for us we gain power to love each other. As the Bible puts it: "We love because he first loved us."

It is the love of God which saves us from another form of deterioration in standards of relationship with others. The really dangerous person who seeks to serve through Life Line is the "do-gooder." It is the person who gains satisfaction by glowing with a conscious or unconscious sense of superiority over others. From the height of a life free from the problem faced by another, there is a stooping down, almost in condescension, to another person in trouble. And when this mood appears, there rises an imperceptible barrier which restricts self-giving in the truest sense.

How is this fatal mood overcome? It is by a vivid awareness of our own desperate plight and need before God. Who are we from our strength or wisdom to offer aid to anyone? Only by God's goodness, by his forgiveness, do we stand immune at any moment from the sin and the suffering which others know. If we have anything to say or offer, it originates not with us, but with God. We all belong—and this includes the people at both ends of a telephone conversation or on either side of a table—to the fellowship of the forgiven.

It is in the humility which a realization of this fact brings that we are made sufficient for continuing service.

From God, and God alone, is gained the strength by which the most critical standards of all, the standards of the spiritual, are sustained.

Regional Centres

It was in New York that I suddenly saw another direction which future development of Life Line should take. It happened this way.

Convinced that the greater the size of a city, the more advanced the conditions of mass society and the deeper the nature of the human problems, I was presenting the case for the establishment of Life Line in America's largest city.

"You are not suggesting that one telephone number and centre would be enough for New York!" exclaimed one Christian leader with a note of incredulity in his voice. "Why, in this city we would need several for English-speaking people, and others in other languages to be available for minority groups."

I realized how right he was, and then my mind flew back to Sydney and to other cities of equal size. By the end of the century Sydney will probably be a metropolis of five million people. What will that do to Life Line?

On returning home we began to grapple with the issue, and saw that the only solution to large, sprawling ribbon-development-type cities was the growth of regional counseling and community service centres. If eight or ten centres could be selected throughout the city in which a limited Life Line ministry could be attempted, each related closely to the central Centre, this might prove the road forward.

So it was in October, 1966, that ten suburbs, chosen for their significance as regional centres in the life of the metropolis, were asked to send representatives to a meeting. Out of that and a subsequent meeting came the adoption of proposals for regional development.

A plan for the growth of regional centres was adopted on the following basis:

1. That the establishment of Regional Life Line Centres providing counseling and community service be encouraged in strategically placed suburban congregations, to circle the city in the north, west, and south.

2. That any such regional project should be initiated either by a local church or on an ecumenical basis, according to local circumstances.

3. That in either case a close liaison with Sydney's central Life Line Centre should be established and maintained so that services provided by central and regional centres should be complementary.

4. That the financing and direction of any regional centres should be the autonomous responsibility of the local church authorities or those whom they shall delegate.

5. That the specialized twenty-four-hour telephone counseling ministry should be practiced by the central Life Line Centre only, to prevent costly duplication and confusion to the public.

6. That regional centres be invited to develop the type of counseling services most likely to meet their situation. One might have a marriage counselor, another a social worker, another a youth adviser.

7. That in any regional centre a lay volunteer team should be trained for service, and that the standards and requirements of Life Line International should be regarded as a minimum requirement for such volunteers.

8. That the central Life Line Centre could be of assistance to the regional centres in the following ways:

   (a) Twenty-four-hour telephone counseling service

   (b) Mobile trouble team suicide prevention service

   (c) Reference centre for clients for specialized and professional counseling in the following fields:

Marriage counseling	Youth guidance	Psychiatric care
Gambling	Alcoholism	Legal help
Unmarried mothers	Financial guidance	Social work

    (d) Emergency child care

    (e) Food and clothing

    (f) Employment and accommodation.

9. That regional centres could be of assistance to the central Life Line Centre. Apart from direct approaches to a regional centre from its community, the central Centre could refer telephone callers (of that district) to the regional centre nearest to them for:

(a) Pastoral care

(b) Caring Division visitation and befriending

(c) Help in the home

(d) On-the-spot investigation of social distress.

(e) Pastoral and marriage counseling by appointment at the regional centre

(f) Local emergency suicide prevention when distance prevents the central trouble team from getting there on time

Already in Sydney three of the selected regional centres are planning to commence operations. Lay teams are attending training courses and the particular form of service emphasis is being chosen. All of which means that another development of Life Line is under way.

A New Christian Strategy

"They . . . found the man . . . , sitting at the feet of Jesus, clothed and in his right mind." So reads the dramatic climax of the story in Luke's Gospel of the healing of the demented man in the land of the Gerasenes.

These were the words which came to mind as I sat one evening at a church tea meeting at an Australian town some 120 miles across the Blue Mountains from Sydney. The minister had quietly indicated to me a woman sitting at the end of the table. "That's the Life Line woman of several months ago," he had said.

It was about 10:30 one morning that the long distance call came. The caller was a distraught woman who said she was sitting at the telephone with a loaded double-barreled rifle between her knees. Her burdens, she said, were so heavy she could carry them no longer and would end her life.

For thirty-five minutes the telephone counselor wrestled with her despair, then the telephone clicked and she was gone. What could be done at such a distance?

A call to the Methodist minister in the town nearest that lonely farm brought quick action. He called a Christian couple nearest the homestead. The wife called and talked with the woman until her husband arrived. He was able to persuade her to relinquish the gun. Soon afterward the minister arrived and convinced the stricken woman she should accompany him to a local hospital.

Into the life of that woman, during and after psychiatric treatment, came friendship and care from members of the church of that town. New hope and confidence were born in her life. Presently she was discharged and returned home.

Now, there she was, "clothed and in her right mind." The special significance of this incident lay in the potential strategy it revealed for the witness and service of the church in today's society.

What is the role and purpose of congregations of Christians today? Suddenly almost, this question has forced itself to the very centre of the consciousness of the church.

Christians everywhere are asking what is the point of endless acts of worship on a Sunday which have become an end in themselves. To be meeting for the singing of hymns, the preaching of sermons, the sharing in fellowship, does not seem enough. A religion confined within a sacred building, at a special hour on a Sunday, is appearing increasingly futile.

Slowly it is dawning on the minds of countless Christians that the Christian faith is meant to be not a way of religion, but a way of life. In the face of the crisis which has overtaken the church in many places, the truth is appearing that the church which only worships dies.

The neighborhood church is set down in the midst of the needs of modern society. In the city of Sydney, for example, where Life Line has uncovered so vast a volume of human suffering, many churches have claimed there was little they could do in terms of service.

It is nothing short of tragic that communication between the church and the people has broken down. Worshiping Christians do not know where and how they may serve. The people, often in desperate need within the shadow of the church, do not know how to direct their need to the church.

Into the vacuum have come, in Australia, the service clubs. Rotary and Apex accept the responsibility for meeting some district needs and often uncover pockets of suffering within the community. The clubs in turn draw to themselves the idealism and the service potential of men who, had the church been alert, would have expressed their concern for their neighbor there.

Life Line could reestablish many a line of communication between need and the church. With a central telephone number known to a whole community, people have a readily accessible point of reference in the hour of crisis. If the local church would develop a trained friendship and service group among its members, names could be referred back to the local area. In the local church could be found the supportive group needed for full recovery in many a human situation. Referral could, of course, only be made with the consent of the person concerned, but that consent would many times be forthcoming. Friendship, group activities, worship, could all be found within the life of an alert and prepared neighborhood church.

Something would happen within the life of many a local community of Christians if they became the servant church in action. A Life Line strategy linking together people in need and the church through a telephone counseling centre could make possible the emergence of that servant church. It could point the way to a new Christian strategy in a mass society.

A Network of Compassion

A worldwide network of compassion! This is the glorious vision which begins to take shape with the spread of

Life Line and the establishment of Life Line International.

The world is one. The miles which separate land from land shrink in a jet age. Vast already, by earlier standards, is the movement of migrants and the accelerating travel habits of the people. National boundaries, sea barriers, matter less and less. All is but a foretaste of a world where people, needs, experiences will be pressed into one almost indivisible whole.

Worldwide agencies in every human field will become a necessity. In business organization companies with world-wide affiliations are already becoming commonplace. Cables, radio-telephones, Telstar and satellite television will carry more experiences and events to people everywhere. In crime detection Interpol is an established fact.

Human need does not stop at national boundaries. Compassion must not be halted by oceans. In deeds of mercy, ways must be found of letting them flow wherever need runs.

Through radio-telephone there one day came to the Life Line Centre in Sydney a call from Cape Town in South Africa. The centre there, inspired and patterned on the Sydney Centre, had a request to make.

A young South African had come to Sydney. For a time letters were received by his parents in Cape Town. Then they had ceased. A last letter had hinted at the development of a serious sickness. Anxiety had deepened with the weeks of silence. Could Life Line in Sydney supply any information?

It took some days, but Life Line found that young South African in a Sydney hospital stricken with cancer.

There was not much time, but doctors thought he might live long enough to journey homeward.

All arrangements were made at the Sydney end. A nurse was engaged at the parents' request to accompany their son on his last sad journey. From the other side of the Indian Ocean came a cable that he had safely arrived.

A week later came the second message. The end had come. A grateful family cabled to say what it had meant to them that Life Line in Sydney and Cape Town had cooperated in a poignant act of mercy.

Already, at the beginning of 1967, accredited Life Line centres are in operation in Australia, New Zealand, Canada, and the United States of America. In other cities and countries telephone ministries patterned on the Sydney Centre are already operating or are in process of formation. In addition, many, many are the inquiries flowing into Sydney from all over the world as news of Life Line spreads. It is obvious Life Line is but at the beginning of its international adventure.

With the spread of the concept of Life Line will come procedures for interchange of information and methods of meeting needs which arise with the intercountry and intercontinental movement of people. A way could open for the universal expression of neighborly concern.

Life Line could supply that worldwide network of compassion.

A Lifeline from God

Every Australian knows the simple imagery of the lifesaver on the Australian beach. Suddenly a rip develops, a sand bank collapses, and a swimmer is in trouble.

An upraised arm brings the lifesaving team into action as the belt-man rushes to the rescue. In order to reach the drowning man, the lifeline must be thrown. Skillfully, rescued and rescuer are drawn through the waves against the pull of the current. At last the beach is reached. Another life is saved in the endless drama of the Australian surf.

God in Jesus Christ threw out a lifeline to all mankind. This is the fundamental meaning of the Christian gospel. Jesus Christ is God's lifeline. His is the power which can overcome the currents of doubt, the undertow of sin, the waves of sorrow and disaster.

Life Line is built on the Christian faith. It believes that it can reach to the depth of the need of a city, because God in Christ has already found that need and answered it. Faith in what God has done, what God can do, is the inspiration of Life Line.

There is a magnificent sentence in the fortieth psalm which declares what God can do for me and for you. It shows that God has always been the Deliverer-God. In vivid imagery it proclaims the truth that God is able to rescue us all from trouble and despair. Here is what the Bible says: "The Lord . . . brought me up out of an horrible pit, out of the miry clay, and set my feet upon a rock, and established my goings" (Psalm 40:2 KJV).

The lifeline from God lifts us from the depths of depression and despair. *The Lord brought me up out of a horrible pit.* An exact translation of the vivid phrase "a horrible pit" is "pit of tumult." A man who was in conflict, whose life was tense and broken within, found unity and peace.

The lifeline from God delivers from the clammy power of compulsion, the clinging folds of bondage. *The Lord brought me out of the miry clay.*

Pitiable is the life of any one of us trapped by some compulsive habit. Perhaps we share the experience of the chronic gambler, the hopeless alcoholic, the despairing drug addict, the helpless sensualist.

There is hope for all. Through modern psychological techniques, group therapy, and persistent, constant friendship, deliverance can come. The transforming power of God, flowing direct from his heart, is available to match our need. Conversion is a reality. God in Christ can and does set men free. Slowly, painfully, and sometimes even suddenly, we can be drawn upward to freedom, "out of the miry clay."

God provides a rock of security, a place of ultimate trust. *The Lord set my feet upon a rock.*

Every one of us seeks security. We live with vague feelings of dread or specific, recurrent fears. Perhaps we are looking for security in the wrong places. Perhaps we are basing our hope on something which by its very nature can only be temporary. Something can happen and our prop, our stay, is pulled away, and insecurity overwhelms us again.

There is only one security which never passes away: God himself. Possessions are easily swept away; work and achievements can pall; love, even though it be white-hot, can burn down to ashes. The love of God endures. The rock of salvation stands. The presence of God persists even through death. *The Lord set my feet upon a rock.*

God in Christ gives us purpose for living, and a goal at the end of the way. *The Lord established my goings.*

No reason to live! In this bitter comment is the reason why so many lives falter and fail. Life has lost its meaning and purpose. There is no sense of going anywhere, no goal worth the struggle.

Into our emptiness comes the Christian interpretation of existence. From the challenge to grow toward personal maturity comes purpose. God has designed this world as, to quote the poet Keats, a "vale of soul making." God works to fashion from the crude stuff of our personalities sons and daughters of his who are strong and free.

In service for others Jesus points us to a satisfying way of life. In neighborly concern, in grappling with the forces which imprison and destroy human life, God can establish our goings.

A line of deliverance runs out into Sydney from the Life Line Centre because God has thrown a rope of deliverance to us all. It waits only for us to grasp it. Into our lives, now, can come the releasing, saving power of Jesus Christ.

Why do we fail to give the sign of the upraised arm, the confession of our need? We have nothing to lose save our doubt, our depression, our chains, our fear, and our sin.

LIFE LINE INTERNATIONAL

Life Line International, with its Secretariat, is based in Sydney, Australia.

Information can be obtained and assistance given regarding the establishment and conduct of Life Line telephone ministries from the Secretary. Life Line International is the accrediting and affiliating body for all recognized centres.

All inquiries should be addressed to:

> Mr. Eric Adam, Secretary
> Life Line International
> Wesley Centre, 210 Pitt Street
> Sydney, Australia